THE
TITANIC

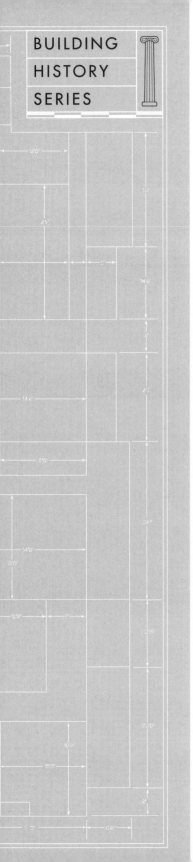

THE
TITANIC

by Nathan Aaseng

Lucent Books, Inc., San Diego, California

Library of Congress Cataloging-in-Publication Data

Aaseng, Nathan.
    The Titanic / by Nathan Aaseng.
        p.   cm. — (Building history series)
    Includes bibliographical references and index.
    Summary: Discusses the design and building of the monster
ship the Titanic, its maiden voyage, and what went wrong on the
fateful night when it struck an iceberg and sank.
    ISBN 1-56006-569-9 (lib. : alk. paper)
    1. Titanic (Steamship)—Juvenile literature.   2. Shipwrecks—
North Atlantic Ocean—Juvenile literature.   [1. Titanic (Steamship) 2. Shipwrecks.]   I. Title.   II. Series.
G530.T6A27   1999
910'.9163'4—dc21   98-31964
                                                                CIP
                                                                 AC

Copyright 1999 by Lucent Books, Inc.
P.O. Box 289011, San Diego, California, 92198-9011

Contents

FOREWORD

Throughout history, as civilizations have evolved and prospered, each has produced unique buildings and architectural styles. Combining the need for both utility and artistic expression, a society's buildings, particularly its large-scale public structures, often reflect the individual character traits that distinguish it from other societies. In a very real sense, then, buildings express a society's values and unique characteristics in tangible form. As scholar Anita Abramovitz comments in her book *People and Spaces*, "Our ways of living and thinking—our habits, needs, fear of enemies, aspirations, materialistic concerns, and religious beliefs—have influenced the kinds of spaces that we build and that later surround and include us."

That specific types and styles of structures constitute an outward expression of the spirit of an individual people or era can be seen in the diverse ways that various societies have built palaces, fortresses, tombs, churches, government buildings, sports arenas, public works, and other such monuments. The ancient Greeks, for instance, were a supremely rational people who originated Western philosophy and science, including the atomic theory and the realization that the earth is a sphere. Their public buildings, epitomized by Athens's magnificent Parthenon temple, were equally rational, emphasizing order, harmony, reason, and above all, restraint.

By contrast, the Romans, who conquered and absorbed the Greek lands, were a highly practical people preoccupied with acquiring and wielding power over others. The Romans greatly admired and readily copied elements of Greek architecture, but modified and adapted them to their own needs. "Roman genius was called into action by the enormous practical needs of a world empire," wrote historian Edith Hamilton. "Rome met them magnificently. Buildings tremendous, indomitable, amphitheaters where eighty thousand could watch a spectacle, baths where three thousand could bathe at the same time."

In medieval Europe, God heavily influenced and motivated the people, and religion permeated all aspects of society, molding people's worldviews and guiding their everyday actions. That spiritual mindset is reflected in the most important medieval structure—the Gothic cathedral—which, in a sense, was a model of heavenly cities. As scholar Anne Fremantle so elegantly phrases it, the cathedrals were "harmonious elevations of stone and glass reaching up to heaven to seek and receive the light [of God]."

Our more secular modern age, in contrast, is driven by the realities of a global economy, advanced technology, and mass communications. Responding to the needs of international trade and the growth of cities housing millions of people, today's builders construct engineering marvels, among them towering skyscrapers of steel and glass, mammoth marine canals, and huge and elaborate rapid transit systems, all of which would have left their ancestors, even the Romans, awestruck.

In examining some of humanity's greatest edifices, Lucent Books' Building History series recognizes this close relationship between a society's historical character and its buildings. Each volume in the series begins with a historical sketch of the people who erected the edifice, exploring their major achievements as well as the beliefs, customs, and societal needs that dictated the variety, functions, and styles of their buildings. A detailed explanation of how the selected structure was conceived, designed, and built, to the extent that this information is known, makes up the majority of the volume.

Each volume in the Lucent Building History series also includes several special features that are useful tools for additional research. A chronology of important dates gives students an overview, at a glance, of the evolution and use of the structure described. Sidebars create a broader context by adding further details on some of the architects, engineers, and construction tools, materials, and methods that made each structure a reality, as well as the social, political, and/or religious leaders and movements that inspired its creation. Useful maps help the reader locate the nations, cities, streets, and individual structures mentioned in the text; and numerous diagrams and pictures illustrate tools and devices that bring to life various stages of construction. Finally, each volume contains two bibliographies, one for student research, the other listing works the author consulted in compiling the book.

Taken as a whole, these volumes, covering diverse ancient and modern structures, constitute not only a valuable research tool, but also a tribute to the human spirit, a fascinating exploration of the dreams, skills, ingenuity, and dogged determination of the great peoples who shaped history.

IMPORTANT DATES IN THE BUILDING OF THE *TITANIC*

One of the Titanic's steam engines.

1786
John Fitch launches the world's first commercial steamship on the Delaware River.

1859
The compound steam engine is invented.

1899
Bruce Ismay assumes control of the White Star company upon the death of his father.

1843
Isambard Brunel's *Great Britain*, the first iron-hulled, screw propeller-operated steamship, is launched.

1775	1800	1825	1850	1875	1900

1838
The *Sirius* narrowly outruns the *Great Western* to become the first steamship to cross the Atlantic Ocean.

1894
William Pirrie takes over control of the Harland and Wolff shipbuilding company.

A painting of the Great Eastern *at sea.*

1858
The *Great Eastern*, the first massive steam-powered ocean passenger liner, is launched.

1902
J. P. Morgan organizes the International Mercantile Marine, which buys the White Star line.

1873
The White Star line suffers its greatest disaster to date when the *Atlantic* sinks, resulting in the deaths of 546 people.

1907
Cunard launches the giant luxury liners *Mauretania* and *Lusitania.* Pirrie and Ismay respond by planning a fleet of three larger, more luxurious liners.

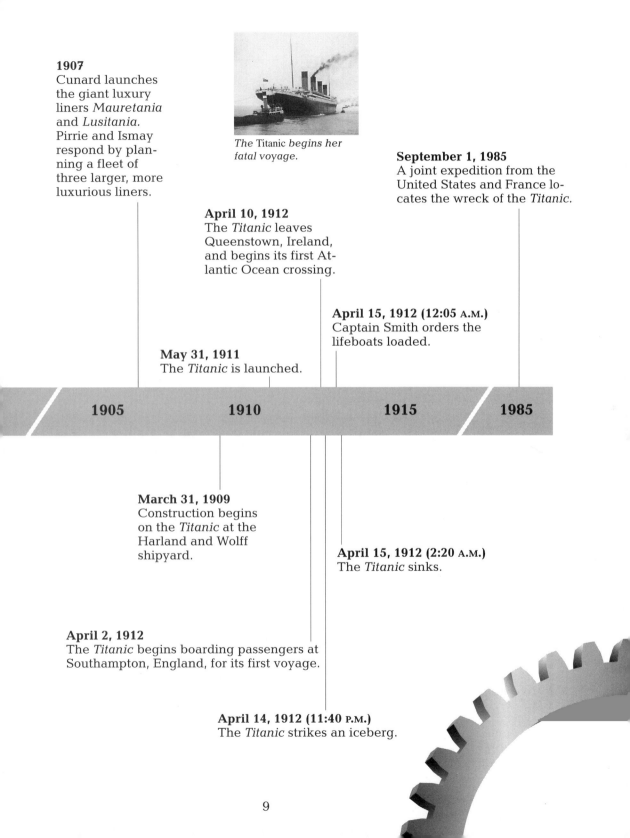

The Titanic *begins her fatal voyage.*

September 1, 1985
A joint expedition from the United States and France locates the wreck of the *Titanic.*

April 10, 1912
The *Titanic* leaves Queenstown, Ireland, and begins its first Atlantic Ocean crossing.

April 15, 1912 (12:05 A.M.)
Captain Smith orders the lifeboats loaded.

May 31, 1911
The *Titanic* is launched.

| 1905 | 1910 | 1915 | 1985 |

March 31, 1909
Construction begins on the *Titanic* at the Harland and Wolff shipyard.

April 15, 1912 (2:20 A.M.)
The *Titanic* sinks.

April 2, 1912
The *Titanic* begins boarding passengers at Southampton, England, for its first voyage.

April 14, 1912 (11:40 P.M.)
The *Titanic* strikes an iceberg.

INTRODUCTION

For Thomas Andrews it was a moment of unspeakable horror.

The *Titanic* was Andrews's masterpiece. He was the designer who had turned his uncle's dream of a fabulous giant ocean liner into a reality. No other ship ever built could match the size or style of the floating luxury hotel known as *Titanic*. Although Andrews was not normally one to boast, he had recently pronounced the ship "as nearly perfect as human brains can make her."[1] But now it lay motionless in the still water, wounded by a shadowy iceberg.

Rumors were flying. The few crew members who had seen or felt the icy water spewing into the ship worried that the damage was serious. Most of the crew and nearly all the passengers believed it was not. After all, this was the *Titanic,* a ship that even the experts claimed was virtually unsinkable.

Along with Andrews, Captain Edward Smith had just completed an inspection of the damage. Captain Smith did not like what he had seen: water rushing into lower boiler rooms, sacks of mail floating as water swirled up the stairways. But he waited for Andrews to pronounce the verdict. Andrews knew his ship so well that, according to observers, "he even seemed to be able to anticipate how the ship would react to any situation."[2] The man was almost obsessed with his creation. Every day he wandered through the liner, evaluating its performance, scribbling notes about how to improve it, complimenting the crew for a job well done. Andrews never read either newspapers or novels. His reading material consisted solely of charts, blueprints, and mathematical tables that littered his room aboard the ship.

DOOMED

A few quick calculations told Andrews the sickening, unimaginable truth: The *Titanic* was doomed. He told the captain that within a couple of hours this magnificent creation would sink to the bottom of the ocean. No power on earth could prevent it.

Andrews had poured his heart and soul into this project. Thousands of workers had labored on the *Titanic* for many months. The ship's owners had invested a huge fortune in it. Now, only four days into its first voyage, all that was going to waste. It was as if they had all worked to construct the most massive, lavish hotel in the world and then towed it into the Atlantic to be dropped into the sea.

"All the News That's Fit to Print."

The New York Times.

THE WEATHER.

VOL. LXI...NO. 19,805. NEW YORK, TUESDAY, APRIL 16, 1912.—TWENTY-FOUR PAGES, ONE CENT

TITANIC SINKS FOUR HOURS AFTER HITTING ICEBERG; 866 RESCUED BY CARPATHIA, PROBABLY 1250 PERISH; ISMAY SAFE, MRS. ASTOR MAYBE, NOTED NAMES MISSING

Col. Astor and Bride, Isidor Straus and Wife, and Maj. Butt Aboard.

"RULE OF SEA" FOLLOWED

Women and Children Put Over in Lifeboats and Are Supposed to be Safe on Carpathia.

PICKED UP AFTER 8 HOURS

Vincent Astor Calls at White Star Office for News of His Father and Leaves Weeping.

FRANKLIN HOPEFUL ALL DAY

Manager of the Line Insisted Titanic Was Unsinkable Even After She Had Gone Down.

HEAD OF THE LINE ABOARD

J. Bruce Ismay Making First Trip on Gigantic Ship That Was to Surpass All Others.

Biggest Liner Plunges to the Bottom at 2:20 A. M.

RESCUERS THERE TOO LATE

Except to Pick Up the Few Hundreds Who Took to the Lifeboats.

WOMEN AND CHILDREN FIRST

Cunarder Carpathia Rushing to New York with the Survivors.

SEA SEARCH FOR OTHERS

The California Stands By on Chance of Picking Up Other Boats or Rafts.

OLYMPIC SENDS THE NEWS

Only Ship to Flash Wireless Messages to Shore After the Disaster.

LATER REPORT SAVES 866.

The April 16, 1912, edition of the New York Times *reports the grim fate of the* Titanic. *Despite claims that the* Titanic *was "virtually unsinkable," an iceberg brought the downfall of the mighty ocean liner.*

But the reality was worse yet. Both Andrews and Captain Smith realized that unless a miracle happened, they were going to die. So would hundreds of passengers and crew who had trusted their lives to Andrews's "virtually unsinkable" ship.

Perhaps no human creation has failed as dramatically and disastrously as Thomas Andrews's *Titanic.* More than eighty-five years after the sinking, the tragedy still haunts and fascinates us. Those aboard the *Titanic* were jolted from absolute smugness and security to face the grim reality that most of them would not survive. They had a little more than two and a half hours to decide how to play out this desperate hand: enough time to demonstrate the best and worst of human behavior, and everything in between.

But in the background of the heartbreaking tales of heroism and cowardice, quick thinking and stunning stupidity, lurks one question: How could such a supposedly safe ocean liner have been destroyed so quickly and easily?

BIRTH OF THE MONSTER SHIPS

The creators of the *Titanic* never meant for it to stand out as the ultimate in shipbuilding. In fact, it was planned as only the second in a series of three monster ocean liners operated by the Oceanic Steam Navigation Company, more commonly known as the White Star line. In the early years of the twentieth century, the company was locked in a bitter contest for the profitable passenger and mail trade across the Atlantic Ocean. Along with its sister ships, the *Oceanic* and the *Gigantic,* the *Titanic* was part of White Star's grand strategy to seize control of the Atlantic shipping lanes.

CHANGES IN THE SHIPPING INDUSTRY

The decision to build three enormous ships came about because of rapid and sweeping changes in the shipping industry in the late nineteenth century. Up until that time, most oceangoing vessels were built of wood and were powered by wind. But these were not the only available alternatives. Engineers had been tinkering with metal hulls and steam-powered engines since shortly after the American Revolution. In the late 1780s, American John Fitch began constructing small riverboats powered by coal-fired steam engines. At about the same time, an Englishman named John Wilkinson successfully floated an iron barge.

But many years passed before these inventions made any impact on the ocean shipping industry. Fitch lost money on his steamships and soon gave up the business altogether. It was not until 1807 that Robert Fulton set up a profitable steamship passenger business by sailing his *Clermont* up the Hudson River from New York to Albany. The *Clermont* was powered by a paddle wheel driven by a coal-fired steam engine.

Meanwhile, thirty-four years passed before anyone transformed Wilkinson's idea into the first iron-hulled ship. Basically, iron was too expensive and shipwrights too inexperienced in its use to make iron-hulled ships practical. There were also serious doubts about its stability in water.

As for steam, it simply could not compete with wind on long ocean voyages. As Robert Albion explained in *Five Centuries of Famous Ships,* "Until more efficient engines were developed, coal and machinery took up so much room that there was not enough space for cargo to meet expenses."[3] Thus, steamships could not make money except on short trips that required little coal. As a result, wooden sailing ships continued to rule the oceans.

In 1838, the *Sirius* and the *Great Western* made an important stride for steamship technology when they competed for the honor of being the first steamship to cross the Atlantic Ocean. The *Sirius* arrived in New York a few hours before the *Great Western,* completing its journey from Ireland in eighteen and a half days. But even though this proved that steamships could make the crossing, it also showed why steamships could not compete with wind. A fast sailing ship could make the trip in about the same

In 1807 Robert Fulton revolutionized the shipping industry with the introduction of the Clermont *(pictured), a passenger ship that was powered by a paddle wheel driven by a coal-fired steam engine.*

amount of time without the expenses of coal and an engine and could carry more than the forty passengers aboard the *Sirius*.

A crucial advance in ocean shipping technology came in 1836, when two inventors independently applied for patents on an invention called the screw propeller. This device consisted of a long shaft with large blades on the end. The steam engine supplied the power that turned the shaft so that its blades propelled the ship through the water. The screw propeller turned out to be far more efficient than the paddle wheel.

Brunel and the Birth of the Modern Steamship

Great Britain's Isambard Brunel, regarded by many as the greatest engineer of the nineteenth century, happened to see a small craft driven by a screw propeller while he was designing a steamship for ocean travel. Brunel recognized this as an improvement over the paddle wheel ship he was designing. He also calculated that the larger the ship, the smaller the proportion of its

WHO REALLY INVENTED THE STEAMBOAT?

Although Robert Fulton gained fame as the inventor of the steamboat, John Fitch beat him to the idea by nearly two decades. The son of a Connecticut farmer who was too poor to provide any schooling for his son, Fitch worked as a gunsmith, a surveyor, and a clockmaker. In the mid-1780s, he was suddenly seized with the notion of building a coach powered by steam instead of horses. After considerable tinkering with the idea, he saw that a steam-powered boat was far more practical. Fitch patterned his steamboat after Indians paddling a canoe. His steam engine drove twelve paddles, six on each side. The paddles dipped in and out of the water, one side at a time.

On July 27, 1786, Fitch tested his first creation, which chugged along for a short distance at about three knots. Over the next four years, he improved the performance so that his boat could travel over eight knots for many hours. Fitch then set up the world's first steamboat passenger service, shuttling along the Delaware River between Philadelphia, Pennsylvania, and Trenton, New Jersey. Unfortunately, he was compet-

space that would be taken up by fuel and engine requirements. Therefore, larger steamships would be more economical to run.

Large wooden ships, however, had a well-earned reputation for being rather fragile. It appeared shipbuilders had approached the size limit of wooden ships. While this problem was churning in the back of Brunel's mind, he observed a small paddle wheel steamship with an iron hull. Most shipbuilders did not believe that a ship with an iron bottom could provide the stability of a stout wooden hull. But Brunel became intrigued by the possibility that iron hulls had the strength to support the structure of ships larger than those currently on the seas.

Putting the two innovations together, Brunel designed an iron-hulled ship driven by a screw propeller. Weighing in at 3,270 gross tons and stretching out to more than 322 feet in length, Brunel's *Great Britain* was much larger than any other ship in operation. It was launched on July 19, 1843, and made two successful round-trip crossings of the Atlantic. Unfortunately

ing against a well-established stage coach service that could make the journey more quickly. Unable to attract enough passengers to support his venture, Fitch had to abandon it. He traveled to Europe in 1793 with the hope of making the influential and wealthy contacts he needed to succeed in business. But he died in 1798, so poor and unheralded that he was buried in an unmarked grave.

Fulton, on the other hand, had the luxury of a partnership with the prosperous and distinguished Robert Livingston. After spending twenty years in Europe trying to advance his ideas for underwater mines and exploding submarines, he returned to the United States in 1806 with a plan for a steamboat service. His *North River Steamboat of Clermont*, launched on August 9, 1807, actually traveled little more than half the speed of Fitch's earlier boats. But Fulton was a well-financed and clever businessman. He made his New York–Albany passenger service along the Hudson River into a success that put him in many history books as the originator of the steamboat.

The S.S. Lewis, an early example of a steamship powered by a screw propeller, sits in the dry docks in Charleston, South Carolina. The invention of the screw propeller soon made paddle wheels obsolete.

for Brunel, a piloting mishap caused the *Great Britain* to run aground off the coast of Ireland in 1846. While the misfortune caused Brunel severe financial hardship, it inadvertently proved the strength of the iron hull. For eleven months, the grounded ship stood up to the merciless pounding of the waves before it was finally freed from the rocks.

THE FIRST MONSTER SHIP

Brunel tried to rebound from the setback with an even more ambitious project. He dreamed of building a steamship so large and fuel-efficient that it could carry all the coal it needed to sail from England to the Far East. In 1854, he set about making this dream come true.

The *Great Eastern* took several years to build, and then its launching was delayed for two months because it was too heavy to move into the water. On January 31, 1858, the massive ship finally floated into the Atlantic. One historian described the *Great*

Eastern as a "combination of bold imagination and engineering skill on the one hand and of economic miscalculation and hard luck on the other."[4] At 18,914 gross tons, this ship was nearly six times the size of the *Great Britain.* Eight engines fueled by 112 furnaces provided the power to move the giant vessel. The *Great Eastern* had room for four thousand passengers, ten times as many as the next largest passenger ship. Unfortunately, the grounding of the *Great Britain* drained so much of Brunel's finances that he was never able to set up his ambitious route to the Far East. The *Great Eastern* lost money hand over fist, beginning with its first voyage. On May 17, 1860, it set sail across the Atlantic with only thirty-five passengers rattling around in its vast interior.

Large crowds gathered to see this great curiosity whenever it came into port. The owners who bought the ship from the financially strapped Brunel tried to take advantage of the public curiosity by charging admission to tour the ship. But they continued to lose money. Eventually, they abandoned the passenger trade. The *Great Eastern* performed its most useful service by laying the first transatlantic cable, in 1862. But it never escaped the mountain of debt it ran up. The *Great*

Engineering legend Isambard Brunel furthered shipping technology with his designs for mammoth ships.

Eastern changed owners seven times and all seven went bankrupt. By the end of its career, it was reduced to a degrading stint as a floating billboard for a department store. In 1889, the ship was finally broken up.

The *Great Eastern* was years ahead of its time. Smaller, wooden sailing ships continued to dominate the ocean throughout the 1860s. Even British warships built to run on steam engines continued to use sails as well so that their cruising range would not be limited to their coal supply. But Brunel had foreseen the

Curious tourists marvel at the sight of Brunel's second enormous steamship, the Great Eastern. *Although a financial failure, the great ship signaled the future of shipping.*

future of ocean liners and provided a blueprint for what was to come. In fact, more than forty years would pass before a larger ship sailed the ocean.

THE ATLANTIC PASSENGER TRADE

One of the main influences in the adoption of steam and steel over sails and wood was the passenger trade across the Atlantic. This business provided a huge source of income for shipping companies in the nineteenth century. American wooden sailing ships, such as those of the Black Ball line, had dominated the trade in the early part of the century when 4 million immigrants sailed to the Americas from Great Britain alone. British firms had been unable to compete with American shipbuilders, who could obtain wood for their ships far more easily and cheaply than could their British rivals.

But the tide turned in favor of British shipbuilders in the middle of the century. The price of wood rose while the cost of iron dropped, and engineers developed steel, which proved a more sturdy construction material than iron. The British were eager to press their advantage in the iron industry and in steam engines, especially with the United States preoccupied with the costly and destructive Civil War. When the war ended in 1865, the United States grew prosperous and continued to expand.

Millions of Europeans, tired of scratching out a bare living, were eager to move to this new land of opportunity. On the other hand, tens of thousands of disillusioned and homesick Europeans who had come to the United States now wanted to return home. There were also a growing number of wealthy people interested in traveling between the United States and Europe. These people wanted to travel in style and were willing to pay handsomely for luxury. This demand for passage, added to the money that could be made from the transatlantic mail route and small cargo delivery, sparked a fierce competition among shipping companies. With its dominance of the steam engine and the steel industry, Great Britain was poised to take advantage of a revival in the Atlantic passenger trade.

ATTRACTING PASSENGERS

Ocean line competitors had only two basic options for attracting customers. They could offer better service than their rivals or lower prices. Better service meant one of three things: The companies could guarantee a more reliable schedule, they could shorten the time of the trip, or they could provide larger and more comfortable accommodations for the voy-

Immigrants crossing the Atlantic Ocean gaze upon the Statue of Liberty. The passenger trade across the Atlantic boomed in the late nineteenth century.

age. As it happened, the new technology had arrived just in time for shipbuilders to accomplish all of these goals.

Steamships could offer better reliability than sailing ships because their speed was more predictable. A sailing ship's speed depended on the amount of wind available. Because of this, no one could know how long the ship would take to cross the ocean on a particular voyage. Arrival times were only a rough guess that could be off by several days. Steam engines, whose speed was more constant, provided a more reliable means of transportation for schedule-conscious passengers.

Innovations in steam power gradually gave steamships greater speed than sailing ships. Furthermore, inventors designed safer, more efficient engines that increased the distance which steamships could travel at these high speeds. Steam engines of 1850 roughly doubled the sailing range of steamships a decade earlier. The compound steam engine, introduced in 1859, was about twice as efficient as those engines. Because it used less coal and took up less passenger and cargo space, this new engine became more practical for ocean voyages. With Great Britain leading the charge, shipyards began abandoning wood and sails for steam and iron in the 1870s. By 1890, wooden sailing ships were used only for very long cargo runs from Europe or the eastern United States to the Far East.

Finally, new steel-working technology made possible ships of enormous size. Such ships could not be made out of wood. There simply were no trees available of the size and strength needed to provide structure and support for enormous ships. However, there seemed to be no limit to the size of a ship that could be made with the stronger and more flexible steel.

In other words, by switching to steel and steamships, the British could build faster, larger, more reliable ships.

THE QUEST FOR SPEED AND SIZE

No one in the shipping industry, however, could rest on their laurels. Various British companies and powerful rival European firms engaged in a cutthroat competition for the Atlantic passenger trade. By the end of the 1870s only eleven major companies remained in the running. As each experimented with ways to lure customers, they built larger, faster, more luxurious ocean-going vessels. In 1874, the largest operating ocean liner weighed 4,555 gross tons. Ten years later, passenger ships topped 7,700 gross tons. By 1893, shipyards were turning out ocean liners of nearly 13,000 gross tons—almost three times the size of the largest ships of twenty years earlier (with the exception of the *Great Eastern*). Yet these great vessels could churn through the water faster than the smaller ships of the past.

As the ocean liners grew larger and more expensive to build, even some of the established companies could not afford to remain in the competition. By the turn of the century, two British shipping lines, White Star and Cunard, stood at the top of the heap, along with Hamburg-Amerika and North German Lines of Germany. In 1898, White Star raised the stakes by producing the *Oceanic*. At 705 feet in length, the *Oceanic* was longer than any previous ocean liner in history, and at 17,274 gross tons, just a little lighter than the *Great Eastern*. Meanwhile, the German companies claimed the distinction of owning the fastest liners on the seas.

In 1907, Cunard made its move. It had been experimenting with a new type of engine called a turbine. Whereas previous engines operated by means of pistons pushing up and down in steam cylinders, this engine used high-speed jets of steam to spin fans that turned the propeller shaft. The experiments were so successful that Cunard installed the engines in two new ships, the *Lusitania* and *Mauretania*. Backed by a subsidy from the British government, which was interested in huge, fast ships to transport troops in the event of war, Cunard built both of these ships to be nearly twice the size of White Star's *Oceanic*. Despite their size, the two ships took turns breaking the speed record across the Atlantic. The *Mauretania* proved to be slightly swifter in the end. Its record average speed of more than twenty-four knots on an eastbound Atlantic crossing stood for twenty-two years.

PIRRIE PONDERS THE CHALLENGE

Cunard's triumph posed a problem not only for White Star but also for Lord William Pirrie, who ran the highly respected Harland and Wolff shipyard. Pirrie was concerned about Cunard because of an alliance he had made. In order to secure business for his shipyard even in hard times, he had offered secret "favored client" contracts to certain large shipping companies. When a favored client wanted a new ship built or needed repairs on an existing ship, Harland and Wolff pushed these orders ahead of whatever other work it had to do. Over the years, this had brought Harland and Wolff a steady stream of business from these big companies, one of whom was White Star. In fact, their relationship was so close that in all its years of existence, White Star never ordered a ship from any other shipyard. But the alliance also meant that if Cunard thrashed White Star in the passenger shipping wars, Harland and Wolff could lose its best customer.

Pirrie had been worried about White Star's health ever since the death of the company's owner, T. H. Ismay, in 1899. Ismay had brilliantly steered the company to success from its early days as a small shipping line transporting British emigrants to Australia. Control of the company had then passed to his son, J. Bruce Ismay. Pirrie questioned whether the younger Ismay had the experience or skill to fight off White Star's competitors.

A strong-willed man who thrived on public approval, Pirrie refused to accept defeat. Nor was he about to stand by and hope that White Star would come up with an answer to Cunard's mighty twin ships. Pirrie liked to solve problems himself, so much so that those who worked for him described him as a dictator.

A painting depicts the turbine-powered Lusitania, *one of two British ships to pioneer the new engine type. The invention of the turbine allowed ships to exhibit both speed and bulk.*

WILLIAM PIRRIE: THE *TITANIC'S* FOUNDER

William Pirrie was the son of Irish immigrants who settled in Quebec, Canada, where William was born in 1847. His father died when William was young, prompting the boy and his mother to return to the Northern Ireland city of Ulster. There, the fifteen-year-old Pirrie found work as an apprentice to the shipbuilding and engineering firm of Harland and Wolff.

As the company prospered, Pirrie impressed Edward Harland with his sharp business sense and leadership skills. When Pirrie was only twenty-seven, Harland offered him a position as partner in the company. Upon Edward Harland's retirement in 1894, Pirrie took control of Harland and Wolff. Under his leadership, it grew into the largest shipbuilding firm in the world.

Pirrie and his company survived the *Titanic* incident with no major, long-term difficulties. In fact, Harland and Wolff actually profited from the disaster. The new ship safety regulations that governments required in the wake of the *Titanic* controversy sent most ships back to the docks for improvements. Harland and Wolff performed a substantial share of this business. More than a decade after the sinking of the *Titanic,* Harland and Wolff remained Great Britain's largest shipyard, accounting for well over one-third of the total tonnage of ships produced in that country.

As he mulled over a strategy for topping Cunard's latest success, he saw that he did not have much choice. Speed was expensive. The only way to get it was to beef up the engines and cut down on passenger space. Bigger engines cost more money. Cutting down on passenger space reduced the amount of income per trip. Pirrie found that increasing a ship's speed by enough to save twelve hours on an Atlantic crossing would require cutting the company's earnings by 40 percent. Any shipping line that tried that would be cutting its own throat.

Therefore, Pirrie concluded that the only way to challenge Cunard was to build a bigger ship—a much bigger ship. A monster ship, one that dwarfed even Cunard's *Lusitania* and *Mauretania,* could provide space for more paying passengers, as well as more room and luxuries to attract free-spending first-class passengers. Pirrie's thinking was not revolutionary by any means.

In their struggle to surpass Cunard, Harland and Wolff shipbuilder William Pirrie (right) and White Star mogul J. Bruce Ismay (left) conceived a line of immense and extremely luxurious ocean liners.

Everyone in the ocean liner business knew that the easiest way to increase profits was to build bigger ships that could carry more passengers. According to an industry historian, "Once the technology was available, the growth in the size of ships was unstoppable, whether anyone wanted them or not."[5] The only question was, How big could these ships be built before they became unwieldy and impractical?

PIRRIE'S GRAND DREAM

Instead of gradually increasing his ships' size and evaluating their performance before moving on to the next level, Pirrie decided to go for broke. He envisioned a fleet of ships far grander than anyone had ever proposed. The initial cost of building a fleet of giant ships would be enormously expensive, but that did not worry Pirrie. He knew full well what few people in the world realized, that White Star was owned by a man who had more money than he knew how to spend.

LUSITANIA: ANOTHER SUPERLINER MEETS A TRAGIC END

Ironically, one of the *Titanic*'s major rivals in the ocean liner business met a similar fate. When the *Lusitania* first set sail in 1907, it created nearly the same stir as the *Titanic* did five years later. It was the first ship to surpass the size of the legendary *Great Eastern.* Despite its great bulk of over thirty thousand tons, it was long and slim, and built for speed. Although not quite as fast as its sister ship, the *Mauretania,* the *Lusitania* could surge through the seas at a top speed of thirty knots. Like the *Titanic,* the *Lusitania* boasted of luxury passenger quarters, including such novel features as hot and cold running water, individual bathrooms, and cabin phones.

By the time it prepared to set sail from the United States in early May 1915, it had completed more than a hundred round-trip crossings of the Atlantic. There was some concern that the *Lusitania* might be in danger. After all, World War I was in full swing and Germany considered British ships as fair targets for its submarines. Germany even took out newspaper ads warning people not to sail on the *Lusitania.* But hardly anyone took the warnings seriously. According to A. A. Hoehling in *Ships That Changed History*, the *Lusitania*'s captain scoffed, "It's the best joke I've heard in many days, this talk of torpedoing." He believed his ship could simply outrun any submarine that came near. The public agreed with him. Despite the warnings, more than 1,200 people boarded the ship for the ocean crossing, including 124 children.

The captain neglected to consider that, because of wartime coal shortages, the *Lusitania* had to shut down six of its twenty-five boilers. Its top speed now was down to about twenty knots. Nor would any speed help if it came upon a submarine unawares. That was what happened on May 7, 1915, as the ship sailed within sight of the Irish coast. An undetected German submarine fired a single torpedo. Within eighteen minutes, the *Lusitania* disappeared under the waves. Of the 1,959 people aboard, 1,198 died. Among the dead were 94 children, including 31 of the 35 infants on board.

Prior to the sinking of the *Lusitania,* the U.S. government firmly promised to stay out of the war in Europe. But the horror of the tragedy helped turn American public opinion against Germany. It was a major factor in prompting the United States to declare war on Germany on April 2, 1917.

Wealthy American financier J. P. Morgan, the secret owner of the British-run White Star shipping empire.

That man was legendary American businessman J. P. Morgan. Since the British people balked at allowing rich Americans to buy key British industries, Morgan hid his involvement in a complex financial scheme. Instead of openly buying White Star himself, he organized a separate company in 1902 called the International Mercantile Marine. This company then bought a controlling interest in White Star. To disguise the deal from the public, all White Star ships continued to sail under the British flag and all were commanded by British officers. Morgan also kept Bruce Ismay in place as the company's director.

Knowing that Morgan had the money to pay for the daring gamble on monster ships, Pirrie arranged a meeting with Bruce Ismay in 1907. There, the two worked out the details of Pirrie's proposal. If the bold plan was successful, not only could White Star answer Cunard's challenge, it might even be able to drive its main competitor out of business.

Building the *Titanic*

After the turn of the century, competition for the honor of operating the most comfortable, luxurious ocean liners was fierce. In
fact, there were schools specifically created to train interior designers in the art of furnishing these ships. One of these designers boasted, "We may, without exaggeration, liken the saloons
of our best ocean liners to the halls of kings' palaces."[6]

The White Star line and the Harland and Wolff shipyard took
special pride in their reputation for stylish ocean travel. White
Star had been the first to install cabins in the middle section of
the ship. Previously, steamship cabins had been placed on the
less stable forward and rear ends, a tradition started when paddle wheels and engine works took up so much midship space.
White Star had also been the first to extend a fancy saloon all the
way across the width of a ship.

Now with its three giant ships, White Star insisted on providing comfort for passengers even beyond the current lofty
standards. When the *Olympic,* the first of the three, took shape
at the Harland and Wolff yard in 1910, it was nearly 50 percent
bigger than even the massive *Mauretania* and *Lusitania.* This
gave it room to provide spacious cabins. Even the third-class
cabins, which contained four bunks, were far larger than such
passengers were used to. One of the *Olympic's* prized features
was the first swimming pool ever built aboard a ship.

The Ultimate in Traveling Luxury

In designing the *Titanic,* which began construction even before
the *Olympic* was finished, Thomas Andrews and his assistants
were determined to build something even more lavish than the
Olympic. They copied many of the *Olympic's* prized features,
such as the swimming pool and large cabins. But everything was
designed with an extra flair, sparing no expense.

White Star's *Titanic* would dazzle its first-class passengers
with a breathtaking grand staircase that rivaled the foyer of the
finest palace. Carved from the finest oak, its polished finish would

gleam under the light of a glass rotunda. The lounge was patterned after France's famed Palace of Versailles. Included
among the ship's luxury dining rooms would be a genuine
French sidewalk cafe.

The *Titanic* would boast of first-class suites that were a full
fifty feet long. These would include private promenade decks
where passengers could walk and enjoy the ocean view. Whereas the *Olympic*'s promenade decks had been outdoors and
exposed to wind, rain, and cold, the *Titanic* would have decks
enclosed in glass. Unlike the *Olympic*, the *Titanic*'s floor would
be covered with plush carpeting.

The *Titanic*'s designers called for first-class rooms furnished
in a style that would provide even the wealthiest patrons with all
the comforts of home. Each suite would be decorated in a different period style. Some would even be furnished with fireplaces.
Ship construction would be hidden behind wood-paneled walls
that were decorated with expensive tapestries, ivy, climbing
plants, and even palm gardens. Passengers would be able to

The magnificence of the Titanic*'s grand staircase included its fine oak, luminous polish, and
ornate details. The staircase was just one of many luxuries aboard the famed ocean liner.*

wash in sinks with marble tops and sleep in beds anchored by polished brass bedposts. Elegant windows would replace the small, round portholes of most ocean liner cabins.

Passengers would drink from marble drinking fountains and eat off fine china with silver place settings. Even second-class passengers would be served on fancy blue-and-white china. First-class customers could work out in a gym equipped with stationary bikes and rowing machines (an idea borrowed from German ships) or play a racquetball game called squash, complete with a professional instructor. They could also relax in a Turkish bath.

The *Titanic*'s designers decided to provide storage space for relatively new toys of the rich—automobiles.They even called for the ship to be equipped with its own hospital and modern operating room. Then, before the shine wore off this sparkling jewel of the ocean, White Star would float out an even more elaborate monster ship—the *Gigantic*.

After a busy day aboard the Titanic, *passengers could steal away to the Turkish bath, where they could lounge in lavish chaises.*

DESIGNING FOR SAFETY

The main selling point of the *Titanic* would be its spectacular size and luxury. Steamship safety was not a major source of concern to the White Star line and its builder, Harland and Wolff, as they set out to design the *Titanic*. Shipbuilding technology had advanced to the point where serious sailing accidents on the Atlantic Ocean were almost unknown. In the years between 1892 and 1902, steamships had carried 3.25 million passengers with a combined loss of seventy-three people. Since that time, only nine of the more than 6 million passengers who had sailed the Atlantic had lost their lives. White Star's record was even better. In the past decade it had lost only two of the 2 million passengers it had ferried across the Atlantic. The company could proudly proclaim to customers that they faced no more than a one in a million chance of a fatal accident at sea.

Still, safety was not something a passenger service could take for granted. White Star did not have to go back far in its history to find a tragic stain on its record. In 1873, the White Star luxury liner *Atlantic* had run short of coal on its westbound trip

HOW THE *TITANIC* GOT ITS NAME

The White Star line had a long-standing tradition of having its ships' names end with the suffix "ic." When considering names for his fleet of monster ships, William Pirrie looked for names that described the size and grand scale of his venture. *Olympic* took its name after ancient Greek mythology. Olympic refers to the gods, led by Zeus, who ruled the universe from Mount Olympus. The ship's name had nothing to do with the Olympic Games, which had only recently been revived on a small scale.

An American friend of Pirrie's, David Banks, suggested another name that originated in Greek mythology. The Titans were another group of immortals who ruled before Zeus and his gods overthrew them. One of the most famous Titans was Atlas, who was doomed to carry the earth through the heavens on his enormous shoulders.

The Titanic *in the last stages of completion at Harland and Wolff's fitting-out basin.*

from Europe to New York. Trying to make a run for the nearest port of Halifax, Nova Scotia, it had been stranded and broke up in the waves before help arrived; 546 lives had been lost. No one wanted even a chance of such a thing ever occurring again.

Thomas Andrews was even more concerned with safety than were most influential people in the shipping industry. One worker at Harland and Wolff recalled a scene typical of Andrews in his early years at the shipyard: "Saying that married men's lives are precious, [he] orders back another from some danger-ous place and himself takes the risk." [7] With the kind and hu-mane Andrews in charge, the *Titanic*'s designers went to great lengths to make the ship as safe as was economically possible.

Titanic's main safety feature would be simply its size. A ship so large and powerful had little to fear from the most common danger to ocean ships—other ships. Nor was it likely to suffer any notable damage from even the most severe winds and high waves.

In addition, the *Titanic* designers included state-of-the-art safety features that would protect the ship in any other conceiv-able emergency. Plans called for the ship to be built with a dou-ble bottom. Both bottoms would be constructed of steel heavier and thicker than had ever been put into ocean liners before, with the outer layer alone a full inch thick. The entire ship's structure would have a greater proportion of steel than any pre-vious ship.

Next, engineers would install watertight bulkheads. A bulk-head is a wall that divides one part of the ship from another. This safety feature was first required by the British government in 1854. The purpose is simply to confine any water that leaks into the ship to a small area. If there were no bulkheads, a small leak anywhere could pool throughout the ship until eventually its weight would cause the ship to sink.

The *Titanic*'s designers decided to install fifteen bulkheads that would cross the width of the ship's bottom, separating it in-to sixteen watertight compartments. The captain could seal off these compartments instantly by the flick of an electromagnetic switch that would activate the watertight doors. The six com-partments that housed the ship's twenty-nine boilers, which pro-vided the power for the ship to sail, would each be equipped with its own pumps to clear out water in event of a leak.

COMPROMISES BETWEEN SAFETY AND CONVENIENCE

Titanic's designers ran into a problem, however, in trying to de-sign the bulkheads. For maximum safety, they needed to make the bulkheads rise high above the waterline. If the bulkheads were too short, water filling one compartment could conceivably rise high enough to spill over the top of the bulkhead and into an-other compartment. Ideally, a watertight deck could be installed on top of the bulkheads, making this kind of spillage impossible.

THE TITANIC

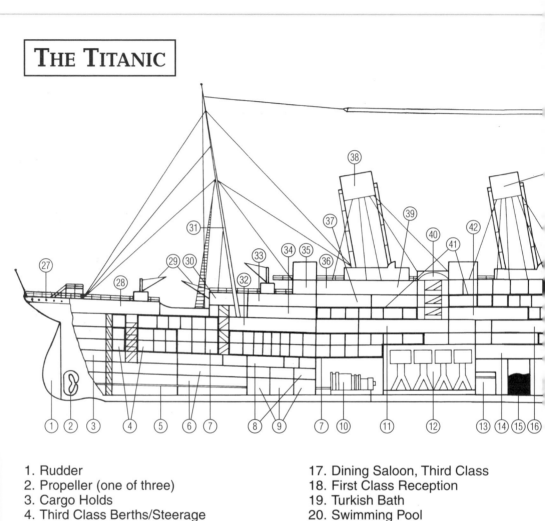

1. Rudder
2. Propeller (one of three)
3. Cargo Holds
4. Third Class Berths/Steerage
5. Propeller Shaft Tunnel
6. Refrigerated Cargo
7. State Rooms, Second Class
8. Ship's Provisions
9. Fresh Water Tanks
10. Steam Turbine Engine
11. Kitchen, First and Second Class
12. Reciprocating (Piston) Steam Engines
13. Boilers
14. Kitchen, First Class
15. Coal Bunkers
16. Dining Saloon, First Class
17. Dining Saloon, Third Class
18. First Class Reception
19. Turkish Bath
20. Swimming Pool
21. Watertight Bulkhead (one of fifteen)
22. Mail Room
23. Squash Court
24. Motor Cars
25. Fire Fighter's Passage
26. Hull (double-bottom)
27. Porthole
28. Smoking Room, Third Class
29. Cranes
30. Second Class Entrance
31. Aftmast

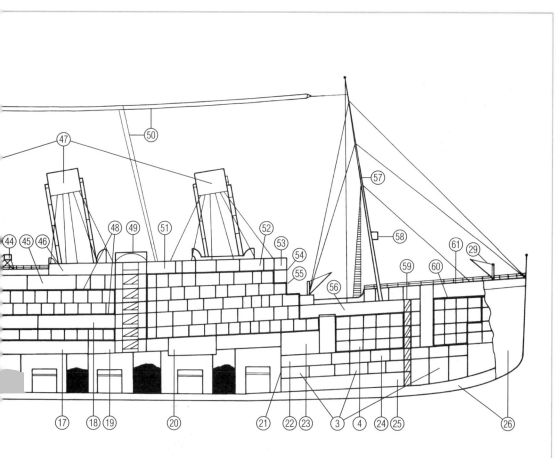

32. Dining Saloon, Second Class
33. Smoking Room, Second Class
34. Library
35. Veranda Cafe
36. Bar
37. Restaurant
38. Dummy Smokestack
39. Smoking Room, First Class
40. Aft First Class Vestibule and
    Staircase
41. Aft State Rooms First Class
42. Maids' and Valets' Dining Saloon
43. Lounge
44. Compass Platform
45. Writing Room
46. Gymnasium
47. Smokestacks
48. Forward State Rooms, First Class
49. Forward First Class Grand
    Staircase
50. Marconi Antenna Wire
51. Marconi (Radio) Room
52. Officers' Quarters
53. Bridge
54. Boat Deck
55. Promenade Deck
56. Third Class Open Space
57. Foremast
58. Crow's Nest
59. Hatch Way
60. Crew's Quarters
61. Forecastle

However, doing so would spoil many of the *Titanic*'s finest luxury features. The wide open grand staircase would lose its effect if it had to be cramped between a couple of bulkhead walls. Passage from one part of the ship to the other would be much more difficult for servants and the crew if they had to climb up and over bulkheads along the ship. And designers would have difficulty laying out spacious rooms if they had to work around high bulkheads.

Some sort of compromise had to be made. *Titanic*'s designers settled for bulkheads that rose a few feet above the waterline. They reasoned that even if something somehow punched a massive hole through both of the thick steel bottoms and flooded two compartments at once, the ship would continue to float high enough in the water so that incoming water could not possibly spill over the bulkheads into the other compartments. Because the *Titanic*'s bulkheads, even at this low height, were twice the minimum standard required by law, the designers felt confident that they had not compromised the safety of the ship for the sake of luxury.

This photograph captures the early construction of the Titanic's *hull, which lacked a longitudinal bulkhead that would have increased its survivability.*

For an extra measure of safety, *Titanic* could also have been designed to include a longitudinal bulkhead that divided the ship down the middle along its entire length. This idea, however, was rejected because it would have made the stokers' job more difficult. The stokers were hired to shovel coal into the boilers. Given the safety provided by the bulkheads already in the design, there appeared to be no point in forcing the stokers to carry shovelfuls of coal up a flight of stairs or through doors into the compartments that held the boilers. After all, the fifteen bulkheads already in the plan were more than most ships contained. Thomas Andrews calculated that the *Titanic*, as designed, could sustain damage to any two compartments without danger of sinking. Even if the three most important compartments were all breached at once, the ship could stay afloat for two to three days, easily long enough to get to harbor. Depending on which compartments suffered damage, the *Titanic* could even continue to sail with four compartments flooded. The odds of more than one or two compartments in such a huge ship flooding at once were almost nonexistent. A gash of hundreds of feet would be required to cause such a situation. How could anything rip a hole that huge in so strong a double deck?

As the technical magazine *Shipbuilder* pointed out in a special edition printed in 1911, the *Titanic*'s thick double bottom made of steel, sixteen bulkhead subdivisions, watertight compartments triggered by instant electromagnetic switches, and tremendous size would all combine to make the ship "practically unsinkable."[8]

EXTRA LIFEBOATS VERSUS AN OCEAN VIEW

The *Titanic*'s designers made one other safety compromise for the convenience of their first-class passengers. The original plans called for forty-eight lifeboats to carry passengers to safety in the unlikely event that the ship became disabled. Figuring 60 people to a lifeboat, this would have handled nearly 2,900 people. *Titanic* was designed to carry a maximum of 905 first-class passengers, 564 second-class, and 1,134 third-class. That would have meant the ship would have lifeboat room for all passengers plus most of the 944 crew who would sail with it on a full voyage.

Unfortunately, the only practical place to store so many lifeboats was on the top deck, which also provided the best view of the ocean. Rather than spoil the view, a view that high-paying customers would certainly expect, those in charge of the *Titanic* cut back to thirty-two davits, or cranes, for holding lifeboats. Researcher Michael Davie concludes, "The builders and owners of the *Titanic* changed their minds about lifeboats late in the day."[9] They continued to revise plans until they had cleared away a great deal of lifeboat-cluttered deck space. This left the ship with only sixteen lifeboats and four emergency rafts with a total capacity of about twelve hundred people.

Titanic's owners were not the least concerned that this potentially left upwards of two thousand people without lifeboat space in an emergency. For one thing, it was well within British Board of Trade safety regulations. The law specified that a ship divided into watertight compartments, as the *Titanic* was, could

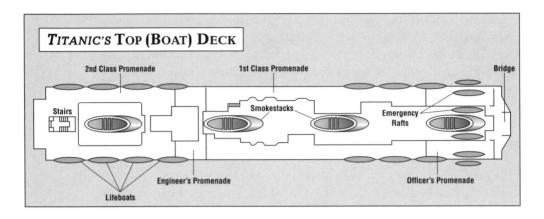

TITANIC'S TOP (BOAT) DECK

2nd Class Promenade

1st Class Promenade

Bridge

Stairs

Smokestacks

Emergency Rafts

Engineer's Promenade

Officer's Promenade

Lifeboats

carry fewer lifeboats than otherwise acceptable. Even in the revised 1911 version of the Board of Trade regulations, *Titanic* was required to provide enough space for only 825 people.

Second, there were good reasons for not carrying lifeboat capacity for every person on board. Industry experts figured that the impact of any collision that could cause a ship to sink would be so crushing that a third of the passengers would not survive it. There would be no sense in providing lifeboat space for them.

Furthermore, loading lifeboats took time. Even a navy crew, who were used to rigid discipline, could seldom load all their lifeboats before the ship sank. A passenger ship crew could never expect to unload nearly 3,000 panicky travelers, many of whom were immigrants speaking different languages, from a sinking liner into boats. A far quicker and more certain way of keeping that mass of people afloat in the water would be to provide each with a life belt. It would take only a matter of minutes for everyone to slip one on. The *Titanic*, then, would carry 3,560 life belts, more than enough for each person to have one. These would keep people afloat until they were picked up by rescue vessels. Even in the ocean, the shipping lanes were fairly well traveled and one could expect help to be fairly near at hand.

All in all, the *Titanic*'s owners were well satisfied that they had done everything possible to design a safe ship that would satisfy the desires of the most demanding first-class patron.

HARLAND AND WOLFF SHIPYARD: BIRTHPLACE OF THE *TITANIC*

The great ship began taking shape at the cramped Harland and Wolff shipyard on the banks of the Lagan River in Belfast, Ireland, in 1909. Harland and Wolff had been in business since 1858 when Edward Harland, a manager for a local ironworks, bought out his employer.

Located twelve miles from the sea along a narrow river, Harland's land was not in an ideal place for him to expand into the construction of oceangoing vessels. But he had used hard-nosed tactics to expand the company into shipbuilding. He created a glut of laborers in Belfast by bringing in shipyard workers from England. Many workers competing for few jobs meant that Harland could pay low wages. If his employees balked at these wages, there were plenty of hungry, unemployed laborers willing to take their places. Harland's strategy was successful and his company began a steady rise into the top ranks of the world's

The cramped Harland and Wolff shipyard before its three building slips were combined into two for the Olympic *and her ill-fated sister, the* Titanic.

shipbuilding firms. In 1864, Harland and Wolff built 30,000 tons of ships. In 1884, they topped the 100,000-ton mark in a single year.

Whenever contract disputes threatened the company's prosperity, the company went back to playing hardball. When the company's riveters went on strike in 1895, Harland and Wolff locked its doors to its eight thousand other workers. Then it persuaded English shipyards to cut back its work forces so that its workers would not be tempted to try and find work there.

The shipyard was a stronghold of Protestant workers in the deeply divided country of Ireland, although Harland had worked hard to prevent this. In the early days, he had promised to close down the shipyard if any Roman Catholic workers were harassed on the job. But he could not protect them or their families from violence at home. Many of his workers took part in efforts to drive out Catholic families, which were largely successful.

Politics continued to dog the shipyard during the building of the *Titanic*. Many workers took sides in a heated dispute over whether Northern Ireland should continue to be ruled by Great Britain or be independent. This led to later speculation that disgruntled Irish workers purposely sabotaged the ship, which was being sailed under the British flag, as an expression of their hatred of the British.

Expense was of no concern to the builders at Harland and Wolff. The designers wanted their ship constructed regardless of the cost, and Harland and Wolff's contract policy of charging White Star for the actual cost of the ship plus a 4 percent profit gave them no incentive to skimp on materials.

THE CRAMPED SHIPYARD

In some ways, however, Harland and Wolff was a victim of its own success. By the time it began work on the *Titanic*, the shipyard had expanded to more than 14,000 workers. The company had expanded from its original 3.5 acres to 80 acres, but in 1899 it had run out of room for further expansion along the riverbank. Since then the company had added on 165,000 square feet worth of shipbuilding shops, 223,000 square feet to its engine works, and had combined three slips into two gigantic slips, specially built to bear the weight of the new monster ships. The result was a cramped, haphazardly laid out, inefficient shipyard.

Despite Harland and Wolff's impeccable reputation and innovative technology, its operation was highly inefficient. A thousand joiners, for instance, continued to ply their trade by hand while other shipyards adopted new machinery.

The woodworking shop and the finishing and decorating shops were a long way from the actual ships, which made getting materials to where they were needed a major hassle.

British shipbuilders had a solid reputation for being the best in the world, and Harland and Wolff was especially noted for being on the cutting edge of industry technology. In 1898, a British admirer stated, "Of all our great firms, there is probably not one which watches more closely the development of machinery and the application of it to their own craft than Messrs. Harland & Wolff."[10] Yet the inefficiency of their operation led to an occasional lapse. As one historian observes, "There were still [at Harland and Wolff] a thousand joiners doing work by hand which in other yards was done on machines."[11]

RED-HOT RIVETS

The backbone of any shipbuilding operation when the *Titanic* began construction on March 31, 1909, was the job of riveting. Riveters had the crucial task of connecting the metal plates so tightly that they would not come apart or leak even under great stress. The connecting device was the rivet—nothing more than a three-inch-long piece of pure iron, about as thick as a thumb.

Before the riveters could do their work, workers in the plate shop had to prepare the plates. Using the latest advances in machinery, they would punch a line of holes near the edge of inch-thick steel plates. These plates would be taken down to the slip where the hull of the ship was being constructed. They would be temporarily bolted in place on the ship's frame at the corners, with care being taken to see that the holes in adjoining metal plates overlapped.

Then four-person teams of riveters would begin performing their monotonous task, often starting at 6 A.M. and working until 5:30 P.M. One worker would heat the rivets until they were glowing red. Using tongs, he would toss the red-hot metal to a second worker who would catch it in a pail and then, using tongs, insert it into the punched hole. A third worker held a hammer in back of the rivet, while the fourth pounded the rivet,

Teams of riveters work on the iron hull of a ship. Their job was extremely important since rivets secured the metal plates that made up a ship's hull, thus keeping the vessel watertight and seaworthy.

AN OCEAN LINER THAT DWARFED THE *TITANIC*

Despite its long-lasting reputation, the *Titanic* was far from the largest ocean liner that ever sailed. In fact, the *Aquitania,* built only a few years after the *Titanic,* tipped the scales at a few hundred tons more. At 901 feet, the *Aquitania* was over 20 feet longer.

Neither of those, however, came close to the size of the mighty *Queen Elizabeth.* It was built in 1940, after White Star and Cunard had merged into one dominating ocean liner company. The *Queen Elizabeth* was over one thousand feet long and weighed in at eighty-three thousand gross tons, about thirty-five thousand more than the *Titanic.*

Once again, though, Great Britain was involved in a war with Germany. In order to keep the *Queen Elizabeth* safe from German submarines, the British quietly sailed the ship to New York and then to the Pacific Ocean. Like the great liners before it, it served as a troop transport ship in time of war.

When World War II was over, the *Queen Elizabeth* was refitted for pas-

Crowds gather near the gigantic ocean liner Queen Elizabeth. *When it was built in 1940, the British liner measured over one thousand feet in length and weighed eighty-three thousand gross tons.*

senger service. It provided spacious quarters for 823 first-class passengers, 662 second-class, and 798 third-class. The *Queen Elizabeth* was paired with the slightly smaller *Queen Mary*—the two ships sailed weekly across the Atlantic, one in each direction. The ships continued to provide service until 1968. By that time, jet airplanes had taken over as the favored method of Atlantic transportation and the era of the great ocean liner was over.

Since then, however, ships have been constructed that dwarf the once-awesome *Titanic.* Current oil supertankers displace over 400,000 tons, which makes them about nine times the size of the *Titanic.*

which would flatten out and widen as it was beaten. As the rivet cooled, it would contract, drawing the metal plates even more tightly together. Riveters had to be careful while pounding. If they did not aim their blows correctly, the rivet could bend and would have to be dug out and replaced. If they did not work quickly enough, the rivet would cool before it was finished. The connection would then be too loose, and again the rivet would have to be replaced.

A riveting team was paid by the number of rivets they put in—two hundred in a day was about average for a good crew. Since the *Titanic* required roughly 3 million rivets in its hull, dozens of crews worked on the project at once, day after day, month after month. Every day, the shipyard echoed with the relentless clanging sound of rivets being battered along the plate edges.

Over the course of many months, the hulking form of the *Titanic* rose above the Lagan River. The skeleton of steel decks rising one over the other seemed like something out of this world. One observer saw it in a sinister light: "It was the shape of a ship, a ship so monstrous and unthinkable that it towered high over the buildings and dwarfed the very mountains beside the water."[12] But a crewman who sailed the Atlantic for forty-three years was moved to declare late in his career, "They can make them bigger and faster, but it was the care and effort that went into her. She was a beautiful, wonderful ship."[13]

SIZE AND POWER

By the time it was completed in the spring of 1911, the *Titanic* was the largest movable object ever constructed by humans. Its four smokestacks, one of which was only for display, soared 175 feet above its keel. The ship stretched out to 882 feet in length and 92 feet in width. Its top deck towered eleven stories above the ground. At 46,328 tons, it was 1,005 tons heavier than its sister ship the *Olympic*, which had been launched seven months earlier.

The *Titanic* was not built to compete with the *Mauretania* and *Lusitania* as far as speed. But it was well powered, with two wing propellers running on compound steam engines and a center propeller run on turbines turned by excess steam from the outer engines. It was capable of fifty thousand horsepower, which would give it a top speed of about twenty-four knots.

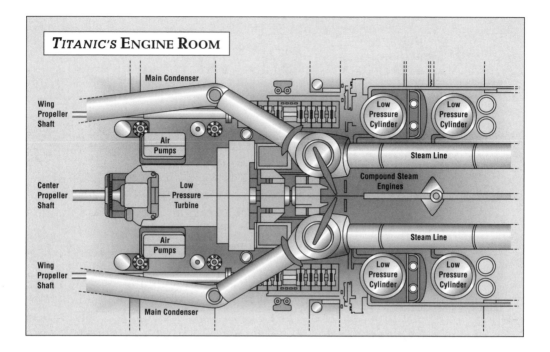

TITANIC'S ENGINE ROOM

Main Condenser

Wing Propeller Shaft

Air Pumps

Center Propeller Shaft

Low Pressure Turbine

Air Pumps

Wing Propeller Shaft

Main Condenser

Low Pressure Cylinder

Low Pressure Cylinder

Steam Line

Compound Steam Engines

Steam Line

Low Pressure Cylinder

Low Pressure Cylinder

On May 31, 1911, a hydraulic ram pushed the *Titanic* off the huge, sloping concrete ramp on which it was constructed into the water. An ominous cloud hung over the proceeding as one of the workers was crushed to death during the launch. But this did not dampen the spirits of the guests of the White Star line. After cheering the great ship into the water, they boarded its sister ship, the *Olympic,* and sat down to an eleven-course dinner as they set sail.

It was a proud moment for William Pirrie, head of Harland and Wolff. The *Olympic* was sailing successfully, the *Titanic* was built, and the *Gigantic* was under construction. Pirrie spoke of moving on to even larger ships, possibly 1,000 feet long and weighing 100,000 tons. His dream of ruling the Atlantic Ocean with a fleet of monster ships was coming true before his eyes.

SEEDS OF DISASTER

Before the *Titanic* could sail with passengers, it had to be tested to see that it was seaworthy. Government officials performed inspections of over one thousand of the ship's components. White Star officials ran the ship through a series of its own tests. All this took time and so the *Titanic* was not ready for its maiden voyage until the early spring of 1912.

TITANIC LEAVES PORT

On April 2, the *Titanic* arrived at Southampton, England, to begin boarding passengers for the first of thirteen scheduled voyages during the year. The ship would stop at Cherbourg, France, and Queenstown, Ireland, to pick up more passengers before setting out across the Atlantic.

First-class passengers paid 870 pounds, or $4,350, for the privilege of riding in this floating luxury hotel. In modern prices that works out to over $50,000 for a ticket. The steep price tag probably accounted for the fact that only 337 customers sailed in first class on the *Titanic,* about a third of its capacity. Most of these were Americans, including some of the wealthiest members of society. Second-class was a little over half full, with 271 passengers, and third-class was at about 70 percent capacity with 712 passengers. These numbers were also slightly low. Third-class passengers were largely immigrants who, at that season, tended to be from the European continent. Such immigrants were more likely to sail from German ports on German liners. The crew numbered 907, including seamen, stokers, bakers, stewards, entertainers, bartenders, waiters, and so on. Altogether, 2,227 people were aboard the *Titanic* when it set sail from Queenstown at noon on April 10.

Both passengers and crew felt supremely confident in the ship as it set out on its ocean voyage. Those who were especially observant noted that the ship tilted very slightly to the port (left) side as it sailed. This may have been because of more coal stored on the port side belowdecks. But all in all, the *Titanic* was

The Titanic *set sail on its maiden voyage on April 2, 1912. It began its journey across the Atlantic Ocean on April 10, carrying 2,223 passengers and crew members.*

remarkably stable. Experienced ocean travelers all agreed that it was the most comfortable ship they had ever sailed upon. They felt secure knowing that they were riding on the largest, strongest ship in existence—a ship built with the best technology in the world. In the words of one passenger, "My feeling was one of total and utter well-being."[14]

But beneath this layer of confidence, the seeds of the *Titanic's* destruction were already being sown.

ARROGANCE

The White Star line never used the word *unsinkable* when advertising its new ship. But company officials considered it to be so. They certainly passed along this attitude to both crew and passengers with their boastful advertising of the ship's strength. One of the crew remarked to a passenger, "God Himself could not sink this ship."[15]

If anyone aboard the *Titanic* had the slightest qualms about the ship's safety, they had only to look to its captain, Edward J. Smith. As the man in charge of the ship, Smith would be expected to provide calm assurance to passengers and crew that all would go well. But Smith went beyond that. He took pride in citing his record of never coming close to a life-threatening situation in his twenty-five years as a captain. This safety record had led him to believe that disasters could not happen. Six years earlier, when piloting a much smaller ship, the *Adriatic*, Captain

CAPTAIN SMITH: ACE OF THE WHITE STAR LINE

Captain Edward J. Smith looked and acted every inch the captain as he took control of the *Titanic.* With his white beard and dignified manner, he projected an image of the confidence and control that passengers found assuring. His record was as impressive as his appearance. Smith was considered the best captain in the White Star line. In his entire career, Smith had never experienced any crisis at sea that put his passengers in danger.

His reputation was money in the bank to his employers. Many passengers of the early twentieth century chose their ship based on who was at the helm. Captain Smith had such a large personal following among ocean travelers that he was known as the "Millionaire's Captain." His ability to attract passengers was one reason why White Star liked to have him take its ships out on their first voyages. The *Titanic* was the seventeenth White Star ship he had commanded in his twenty-five years as captain.

Smith was not only admired by the passengers but greatly respected by those who worked on ships. Susan Wels, in Titanic: *Legacy of the World's Greatest Ocean Liner,* quotes a crew member who described Smith as "a great favorite, and a man any officer would give his ears to sail with."

When he left port with the *Titanic,* Smith was sixty-two years old, in his twenty-sixth year as a White Star employee. In some ways, the trip was his reward for those long years of competent service. Smith was more than ready to retire. Command of the awesome *Titanic* on its maiden voyage was intended as an honor that would allow the old captain to finish his career in style.

Captain Edward J. Smith's flawless record and larger-than-life reputation attracted numerous passengers to the White Star line, but his legendary career would come to an end aboard the doomed Titanic.

Smith was quoted as saying, "I cannot conceive of any vital disaster happening to this vessel. Modern shipbuilding has gone beyond that."[16] If Smith believed that about the *Adriatic,* he was all the more convinced it was true of the much more impressive *Titanic.*

This attitude of invincibility led to carelessness. Captain Smith, the crew, and the passengers all lost sight of the fact that the ocean is a vast, unpredictable, and potentially dangerous place. A good sailor needs to be constantly alert to the many perils it contains.

LIFEBOATS

One of the areas in which this careless arrogance showed most dramatically was in the lifeboat situation. None of the passengers and few of the crew members had any idea how few lifeboats were aboard the *Titanic.* Because of their belief that the ship was unsinkable, most of them would not have cared in any case.

Nonetheless, a responsible crew would have been well informed about the lifeboat equipment and well trained in its use. The *Titanic* crew was neither. Even those officers in charge of filling the lifeboats in an emergency had no detailed set of procedures to follow. Their instincts told them that they could not fill the boats from the top deck. It seemed obvious that the weight of sixty people in a boat unsupported by water would buckle the lifeboat. Even if that did not happen, the weight would surely snap the davits (cranes) that lowered the boats over the side. Therefore, they assumed that the boats would have to be lowered from the top deck to the water before passengers could enter them.

None of them knew that the lifeboats and the davits had been thoroughly tested. Both had shown that they could support the weight of a full load of passengers. Therefore, the boats could be filled immediately, before lowering.

Lifeboat drills were an important part of basic ocean safety. On the White Star line, ships routinely held such drills on Sunday mornings. Captain Smith, however, did not order any such drill on the Sunday morning of the *Titanic*'s voyage, nor at any other time. It could be that he wanted to avoid questions anxious passengers might have when they found out that lifeboat space was available for fewer than half the ship's occupants. At

Lifeboats hang from davits aboard the Titanic. *Since the liner was considered unsinkable, its designers equipped it with only sixteen lifeboats even though forty-eight would have been necessary to accommodate all of the passengers and crew.*

any rate, because there was no drill, none of the passengers knew where they should go if any emergency arose. None of the crew knew how they should proceed to fill the boats.

THE SHIP'S HANDLING

Although Captain Smith had piloted many ocean vessels in his career, including the *Olympic,* he had little experience handling giant ships. No one, in fact, knew much about the handling of such large ships.

Despite his claims of never encountering a problem on the seas, Smith had, in fact, been involved in at least two accidents. In 1899, he was at the helm of the *Germanic* when it capsized in the New York harbor. But a more serious incident took place while Smith was piloting the *Olympic,* just seven months before he took over the *Titanic.* The *Olympic* had collided with the British cruiser *Hawke* while leaving port. The *Hawke's* captain insisted that his ship had been sucked into the *Olympic's* wake. Smith had dismissed the complaint, saying it was the *Hawke's* fault for coming too close. But then while leaving the dock at

Southampton on this trip, Smith's *Titanic* created a wake that pulled the ship *New York* from its dock. The tug was so great that all six ropes holding the *New York* to the dock snapped. As a huge crowd looked on in horror, the *Titanic* came within four feet of crushing the smaller ship. There was no way Smith could blame the *New York* for this near disaster.

These two incidents demonstrated that the giant ships did not handle in quite the same way as other ships. A careful captain would have tested the ship thoroughly in trial runs to become familiar with its handling capabilities. Some captains tested a ship for as long as six weeks before they felt confident they knew what to expect from the ship. Smith, however, took the *Titanic* out for only half a day. His trial consisted of nothing more than steaming into open water, making a few turns, and then heading back to port.

The Titanic *(right) nearly collides with the* New York *(left) after departing from Southampton, England. Mammoth ships like the* Titanic *created enormous wakes that could suck in smaller ships if they were not handled properly.*

Had he more carefully tested his ship, Smith and his assistants would have discovered a couple of dangerous flaws in the ship's engineering. First, it was steered by a fairly crude, hinged rudder. In the words of one ship engineering analyst, "Such a rudder was inappropriate for so large a vessel."[17] This was one reason why the ship responded slowly when the crew tried to change direction.

Even more important was the fact that while the two outside screw propellers had gears that allowed them to be thrown into reverse, the center engine did not. This was not necessarily a glaring weakness—the two outside engines could have given it enough reversing power. Unfortunately, the rudder—the steering mechanism for the ship—was placed directly behind the center engine. A rudder steers through the force of water flowing at an angle against it. But if the center engine was useless when the ship was thrown into reverse, that meant it was directing no water at the rudder. Less force of water meant less maneuverability.

Because the crew had so little hands-on experience operating the *Titanic*, they were not familiar with how to compensate for these problems. If a situation came up where fast, evasive action was required, they would have trouble maneuvering the *Titanic* to safety.

ICEBERGS

The *Titanic* happened to be sailing in one of the worst months for ice in the Atlantic Ocean. Rising spring temperatures spawned roughly a thousand large icebergs per year as well as numerous smaller floating chunks of ice known as "growlers" into the shipping lane. These floating ice islands posed a serious danger for ships. In 1879 the *Arizona* had smashed head-on into an iceberg while traveling at fifteen knots. While the ship had survived, the impact had crushed the forward twenty-five feet of the ship into a crinkled mess.

Captain Smith received plenty of warning that the route he was taking was littered with icebergs. Over a period of three days, the *Titanic* received by telegraph at least seven warnings of a huge ice field, seventy-eight miles long, that lay in its path. Smith is known to have personally seen four of these. As the ship drew closer to the field, the warnings grew more frequent. Just before lunch on Sunday, April 14, Captain Smith handed White

ICEBERGS: INDESTRUCTIBLE ISLANDS

Icebergs occur where massive fields of ice push out from land into the ocean. Chunks of this ice break off, a process known as calving, and float away. About 85 percent of icebergs originate in Greenland, where glaciers are the most active. Antarctica produces most of the remainder. Icebergs from Greenland often float into the North Atlantic shipping lanes, but they have been known to drift over twenty-five hundred miles.

Most icebergs are less than one hundred feet long. But the largest ever reported was two hundred miles long and sixty miles wide—roughly the size of Vermont. All icebergs are far larger than they appear. Because the ice is only slightly less dense than water, they float very low in the water. Only about one-eighth of an iceberg actually appears above the surface.

The ice in an iceberg is so extremely hard-packed that icebergs are virtually impossible to break up. Navies have used dynamite and even bombs without being able to put a dent in them. Eventually, icebergs will melt away in warmer waters and under summer suns, but this may take up to three years.

This deadly iceberg, which is believed to have sunk the Titanic, *weighed an estimated 200,000 tons, making it roughly four times as large as the ocean liner.*

The iceberg that the *Titanic* struck was a fairly large but by no means exceptional one. Experts estimate that it weighed about 200,000 tons, which made it roughly four times the size of the *Titanic*. An iceberg that size would not have budged even had the *Titanic* struck it head-on. In effect, smashing into an iceberg has the same effect on a ship as striking land.

Star president Bruce Ismay a telegraph message from a ship called the *Baltic* that gave a strong warning about ice ahead.

Exactly how Smith responded to these warnings is not known. But he evidently conveyed enough disinterest that his crew did not bother to tell him of a message that came through while he was at dinner that Sunday evening. The message came from the *Californian*, sailing just a few hours ahead of the *Titanic* on roughly the same course. It reported that the ship had just passed three large icebergs.

Smith and his crew did not completely ignore the warnings. The captain ordered a slight course alteration to the south that he hoped might avoid some of the trouble. Lookouts were posted around the clock with instructions to keep a sharp eye out for ice. The crew took the extra precaution of closing the forecastle hatch so that glare from the lights inside the ship would not interfere with the vision of the lookout crews in the crow's nest above.

Smith, however, did not order the one precaution that would have seemed the most obvious when plowing ahead into a field of ice: slowing down. The captain kept the ship running at a speed of greater than twenty knots, very near to full speed. In doing so, he ran the risk that any collision with an iceberg would have a tremendous impact.

Smith's reasons for maintaining such a high speed in the face of iceberg warnings have never been determined. But ocean liner historians note, "maritime professionals did not consider this particularly risky."[18] Icebergs could almost always be

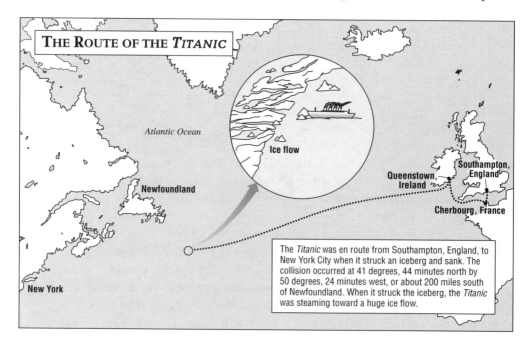

THE ROUTE OF THE *TITANIC*

Atlantic Ocean

Ice flow

Newfoundland

New York

Queenstown, Ireland

Southampton, England

Cherbourg, France

The *Titanic* was en route from Southampton, England, to New York City when it struck an iceberg and sank. The collision occurred at 41 degrees, 44 minutes north by 50 degrees, 24 minutes west, or about 200 miles south of Newfoundland. When it struck the iceberg, the *Titanic* was steaming toward a huge ice flow.

seen at a distance of about three miles, which was plenty of time in which to take action to avoid them. Captain Smith was confident that his crew would have no trouble spotting icebergs. He had been sailing through ice-laden waters all his life and had never experienced any difficulties. There had never been a confirmed case of an iceberg sinking an ocean vessel; the *Titanic*, the mightiest ship ever built, certainly would not be the first. Even the ship's insurers, who like to err on the side of caution, put the odds of an iceberg sinking a ship as a million to one. In view of all this, Smith saw no reason to get skittish. When his crew spotted an iceberg, he would consider slowing down if that was necessary to avoid the ice.

Since the safety of the ship depended entirely on spotters to locate icebergs before they could cause trouble, the ship's officers should have made certain their spotters were well equipped to handle the situation. To its credit, the *Titanic* employed six lookout specialists, more than any other ship in the ocean. The lookouts worked in pairs, in two-hour shifts so that they could be relieved before eye fatigue set in.

Again, however, smug carelessness eroded the *Titanic's* safety. As a safety measure, lookouts on White Star ships were routinely provided with binoculars to help them search the waters. Although these binoculars were often of poor quality, the lookouts had come to depend on them as useful tools. After mounting their perch high in the crow's nest of the *Titanic*, the lookouts were surprised to find no binoculars available. "I asked for the glasses and I did not see why I should not have them,"[19] one of the lookouts later reported. No one seemed to know where they were or why they were missing. Nor did anyone but the lookouts seem to care.

THE WIRELESS

The *Titanic* carried a wireless telegraph unit along with operators employed by the Marconi company. This relatively new invention provided an extra measure of safety for ocean travelers. If the ship ran into any problems, all it needed to do was send a message out over the wireless and any ships in the vicinity would be on their way to help. In addition, the ship could receive up-to-the-minute reports from neighboring vessels on weather and iceberg conditions.

For many of the wealthy passengers aboard the *Titanic*, however, the wireless was yet another marvelous new toy. Many of them felt it was their privilege as paying passengers to make free use of it to send messages home to family and friends. Un-

WAS THE *TITANIC* GOING FOR A SPEED RECORD?

One of the most popular explanations for why the *Titanic* was sailing so fast despite the iceberg warnings was that Captain Smith was trying to set a speed record for the Atlantic crossing. Stories also claim that White Star president Bruce Ismay either suggested, urged, or ordered him to go for the record. The popular 1997 motion picture *Titanic* helped to spread this version of the crossing. But according to Michael Davie, author of Titanic: *The Death and Life of a Legend*, "This notion is and always has been absurd. No ship can go faster than another ship that is lighter and has more power."

The fact is that both the *Olympic* and the *Titanic* were designed for size and luxury, not speed. Their top speed, under ideal conditions, was less than twenty-five knots. The *Mauretania*, which held the Atlantic crossing speed record, *was* designed for speed. It was lighter, slimmer, and better powered. The *Mauretania* was capable of traveling at thirty knots and had *averaged* nearly twenty-five knots on its record crossing. Captain Smith would have been well aware of the difference between the abilities of his ship and that of the *Mauretania*. Rumors that the *Titanic* was gunning for the speed record did not surface until an old surviving crew member suggested it decades after the disaster.

A more likely explanation for the *Titanic*'s speed is that both Ismay and Smith were interested in making good time on the crossing. Ismay was concerned that Cunard was in the process of building ships the size of the *Titanic* with huge engines that could give them greater speed. He did not want a slow crossing that his rival could criticize in promoting its ships.

As for Smith, like pilots of all types of crafts and vehicles, he considered high speed a challenge to both his ability and his courage. Ship captains were often competitive people with a great deal of pride, and they preferred to be thought of as daring rather than timid. Apparently this attitude was especially typical of White Star captains, as Neil Schlager claims in *When Technology Fails:* "Ice fields were a hazard he [Smith] dealt with all the time and robust captaincy was a matter of pride among sea captains, especially those of the White Star line."

fortunately, the range of wireless technology was limited. Once the ship sailed out of the range of European wireless operators, the *Titanic* could communicate only with other ships. *Titanic's* passengers impatiently waited for the ship to come within range of operators on the North American coast.

On Sunday, April 14, wireless operator John Phillips finally made good contact with Cape Race on the southeastern tip of Newfoundland. By then he had a huge stack of messages that passengers had given him to pass on. Phillips worked frantically for most of the day trying to get all these messages out.

The use of the *Titanic's* wireless lifeline to the world for frivolous messages put the ship at further risk. Its harried, overworked operators would be in poor condition to monitor the airwaves for truly important messages.

An operator monitors a wireless telegraph similar to the one employed on the Titanic. *The new invention allowed the* Titanic *to have contact with nearby vessels and, at times, mainland operators.*

A HOMELESS SHIP

Although the *Titanic's* size made it more powerful and stable than other ships, it caused a major problem that Pirrie should have recognized but chose to ignore. Most harbors in the world were simply not designed to handle a ship that large. This would limit the ports to which the *Titanic* could sail should it run into trouble.

Of even more concern was where the *Titanic* could go if it became damaged. There was no dry dock anywhere in North America big enough to hold the ship if it required repairs. The largest one, a navy yard at Newport News, Virginia, was a good eighty feet shorter than the *Titanic*. Harland and Wolff had the only dry dock in Europe that could handle the ship. The captain would have no choice but to somehow make it back to Belfast if there was to be any hope of putting the *Titanic* back in working order. Even if the ship were crippled near the American coast, the captain would be under strong pressure to risk the lives of passengers and crew by trying to limp back across the ocean.

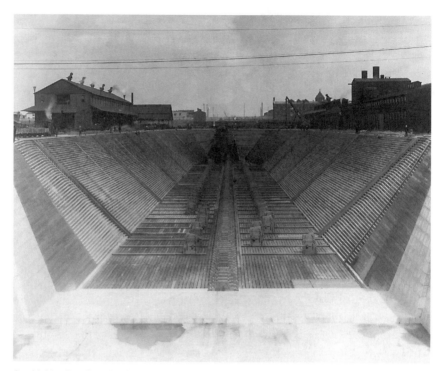

In 1912, the dry dock at the navy yard in Newport News, Virginia, was the largest dock of its kind in North America. Despite its immense capacity, the dock was eighty feet too short to hold the Titanic.

In short, had the passengers and crew not been blinded by the brilliance and sheer size of the great ship, they might have realized that the *Titanic* was not as invincible as it appeared. True, it would take a tremendous string of outrageously bad luck to put the ship at risk. But bad fortune does happen, and a wise person who has responsibility for thousands of lives makes every effort to prepare for it. When bad fortune struck the *Titanic* on the night of Sunday, April 14, 1912, no one was prepared.

THE FATEFUL NIGHT

At 9:20 P.M., Captain Smith sent one last reminder to the men in the crow's nest to "keep a sharp lookout for ice."[20] With that, he headed off for bed, leaving orders that he was to be awakened if any problems arose.

At about that time, a stoker looked out onto the sea after finishing his shift of shoveling coal into the ship's boilers. The water was as smooth as glass, the air deathly still. In twenty-six years at sea, said the stoker, he had never seen a sea so calm. This was the first bad break for the *Titanic* as it steamed toward the great ice field. Lookouts often spotted icebergs, especially at night, by noticing how the waves broke up when they struck the floating objects. There would be no waves to help them this night.

To make matters even more difficult, there was no moon. Although the stars shone clearly through the cloudless sky, they did not give off anywhere near the light of a moon.

MORE BAD LUCK

Another bad break took place a little more than an hour later in the wireless operator's room. John Phillips was nearing the end of an exhausting fourteen-hour day, working through the mound of messages that passengers wanted sent out. As the *Titanic* was still a good four hundred miles southeast of Cape Race, contact with the receiving station there was often faint. Phillips strained to hear the signals.

Titanic wireless operator John Phillips.

Suddenly, a message blared over his headset that was so loud that Phillips thought his eardrums would rupture. The volume of the transmission indicated that the ship must be extremely close by. It was the *Californian* with yet another warning about icebergs. "Stopped and surrounded by ice,"[21] came the message.

With his ears ringing from the blast and with still more trivial messages from first-class passengers staring him in the face before he could quit for the night, the frazzled Phillips lost his temper. He cut off the *Californian* operator with a terse, "Shut up! I am busy." [22]

Had Phillips not been under such enormous stress from the demanding workload and had his ears not been nearly blown off by the volume, he might have relayed the warning the *Californian* was trying to send. Here was a ship, no more than twenty miles away, that had run into so much ice that it came to a complete stop for the night rather than risk trying to weave through it.

"ICEBERG RIGHT AHEAD!"

Shortly after 11:30 P.M., lookout specialists Fred Fleet and Reginald Lee were scanning the sea in front of them. The temperature had dropped rapidly in the past few hours and their breath came in frosty puffs. They were in the final half hour of their two-hour shift and had so far seen nothing dangerous. But all at once, Fleet had the anxious feeling that something was not quite right. Peering into the blackness, he picked up the shadowy shape of an iceberg, not more than a quarter mile away. Immediately, he rang his warning bell three times and grabbed the telephone to the engine room.

"Iceberg right ahead!" [23] he reported.

With Captain Smith asleep, First Officer William Murdoch was in charge of the ship. Without hesitation, he ordered the crew to reverse the engines and turn the rudder hard so the ship would veer hard to port (the left). At the same time, he prepared for the possibility of a collision by pulling the lever that automatically closed the watertight doors in the engine and boiler rooms.

First Officer William Murdoch was in command of the Titanic *when lookouts sounded the alarm. Despite his quick actions, the* Titanic *was unable to avoid the iceberg.*

At the time of the iceberg sighting, however, the *Titanic* was surging through the sea at better than twenty knots. Even the act of reversing the engines would scarcely be able to slow the tremendous momentum of the giant ship. Turning sluggishly, as was its nature, the ship began to veer to the left of the iceberg. The lookouts could see that it was going to be a close call. For thirty-seven agonizing seconds, the great ship drew near the iceberg, straining against its momentum to steer to port. The ship looked as though it was sliding by.

COLLISION

Then it hit. Those in first class, in the upper regions of the ship, felt only a mild shudder or a slight jar. Many of them slept through it completely. To others, the brush with the iceberg was a source of amusement. A couple of tons of ice shaved off the iceberg landed on the ship's deck. Some passengers laughingly collected pieces as souvenirs or to cool off their drinks. Others, nearer the point of impact, heard a grinding sound or, in some cases, something that sounded like metal ripping. Still, there was very little jolt, the iceberg quickly disappeared, and the mighty *Titanic* sat in the water just as it had before the incident. There appeared to be nothing to worry about.

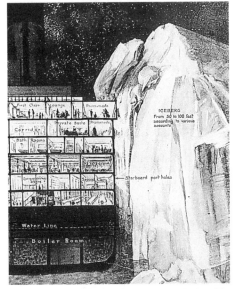

Down in the belly of the ship, however, others had a more frightening view of the encounter. Those third-class passengers with rooms on the starboard bow (right-hand, front) side of the ship heard a frightening crash. In boiler room 6, the whole outside wall of the

A cross-sectional depiction of the Titanic shows the ship colliding with the iceberg. Third-class passengers shouldered the brunt of the collision.

ship seemed to collapse, as if a dam had burst. Workers dashed to safety just before the watertight door slammed into place behind them.

SHOCKING NEWS

Captain Smith sensed something was wrong. After the on-duty crew briefed him about the accident, he summoned Thomas Andrews. The two headed down the stairs to take a brief tour to see where the damage had occurred and how serious it was. Although they were concerned about the condition of the ship at this point, they had no reason to believe the passengers were in any danger. The impact seemed to have been on the starboard bow. Andrews knew better than anyone that the farther forward the damage, the better. While the *Titanic* could stay afloat with any two of its compartments flooded, it could survive even if three of the first five were breached. It could even withstand flooding in the first four compartments. In other words, even if the iceberg had somehow opened a terrible gash more than one hundred feet long in the ship's side, the *Titanic* could continue to sail. There was no reason to suspect that such a mild collision could open a gash anywhere near that large.

The tour, however, told a different story. Andrews found all five of the forward compartments taking water. The pumps in those compartments were steadily losing ground and the water levels were growing higher. Within ten minutes of the collision, water had already risen as high as fourteen feet in the bow (forward portion of the ship). A shaken Andrews calculated that the iceberg must have torn a hole three hundred feet long through the inch-thick steel plating.

From this point, it was merely a matter of time. As water flooded into the ship, the bow would become heavier and sink lower in the water. This would allow more water to pour in the gashes. Soon the tops of the bulkheads in the flooded compartments, which were normally several feet above water, would be below the water level. That meant that water in the flooded compartments would be able to slosh over into the next undamaged compartment further aft. As that began filling with water, the boat would sink lower yet. More bulkheads would slip below the waterline. Water would spill over the tops of these bulkheads into the next compartments, and so on. Finally, the weight of all that water in the compartments would pull the *Titanic* down and it would sink to the bottom of the ocean.

The impossible had happened. The *Titanic* had run into just about the only situation that could sink it—a sideways blow ripping down the length of the ship. It was going down.

THE *CALIFORNIAN*: SO CLOSE AND YET SO FAR

Now that he had lost his ship, Captain Smith's only remaining duty was to save the lives of those on board. Immediately, he sent out emergency messages by wireless asking for help. The *Titanic,* in fact, was the first ship to use the new SOS signal, the international signal for distress.

But once again, misfortune plagued the *Titanic*. The *Californian* was certainly within twenty miles of the dying ship, per-

The Carpathia *(pictured), at fifty-eight miles away, was the nearest ship to respond to the* Titanic's *distress call. Although she steamed at close to full speed, the* Carpathia *would not arrive on the scene for at least four hours.*

haps closer than ten. One *Titanic* officer saw the ship and tried to get in touch with it using a Morse lamp. If alerted to *Titanic's* plight, the *Californian* could have arrived in time to take on many of its passengers. But the ship's crews did not monitor their wireless sets twenty-four hours a day. At 11:30, Cyril Evans shut down his radio aboard the *Californian.* He had been at his post for sixteen hours and, bone-weary, headed off for bed. Another officer, who liked to play with the set when it was not in use, put on headphones. But he had trouble getting it to work and gave up.

As it was, the nearest responding ship was the *Carpathia,* fifty-eight miles away. Because its wireless operator was taking a late-night break, it did not receive the news until 12:25. Even running at full speed, which would be dangerous in this ice field, the *Carpathia* could not arrive for at least four hours.

Desperate to attract the attention of the *Californian,* the *Titanic's* crew set off a series of eight flares that burst into the sky and lit up the night. Officers aboard the *Californian* saw them clearly and suspected that this might be an attempt to call for help. They awoke Captain Lord and asked for instructions. Lord, however, was not certain whether this was a distress signal or a party or something altogether different. He told his crew to signal the *Titanic* with Morse lamps to find out if there was a problem. When they did not detect a response, Lord decided there was no point in getting involved.

DEATH BY EXPOSURE

By this time Captain Smith was well aware that there was going to be a tremendous loss of life, including his own. Even if they could get all the lifeboats and rafts filled to capacity, more than twelve hundred people were going to be left behind. According to Andrews, the *Titanic* would be lucky to last another two hours in the water. It would be sitting on the bottom of the ocean by the time the *Carpathia* arrived.

If the water were warmer, the life belts might be able to keep hundreds of people alive until rescue ships arrived. But the ocean temperature was about 28° Fahrenheit. (The water could be that cold without turning to ice because, although pure water freezes at 32° F, salt water freezes at a lower temperature.) Anyone floating in that water would be lucky to last a half hour before dying of exposure. Only those in a lifeboat could survive long enough for help to arrive.

THE LIFEBOAT FIASCO

At 12:05 A.M. Captain Smith ordered his crew to begin loading the lifeboats. In one way, the *Titanic* was more fortunate than most ships that suffer a major disaster at sea. The collision had caused no serious injuries. It had not tipped the boat one way or the other, causing lifeboats to fall into the water. In fact, although the bow was gradually sinking, the ship was level enough for passengers to begin boarding the lifeboats. The *Titanic* also stayed afloat far longer than most fatally crippled ships, allowing plenty of time to fill the boats.

Unfortunately, the earlier smug assurance about the *Titanic*'s safety spoiled any chance of an orderly evacuation. According to surviving passengers, the crew reacted slowly to the crisis, apparently because they could not believe the *Titanic* was really in trouble. When they finally did take the incident seriously, they found passengers refusing to cooperate for the very same reason. The crew gave them the impression that they were filling lifeboats merely as a precaution. Since most people refused to believe the *Titanic* could sink, the prospect of boarding a lifeboat seemed foolish. Many of them stayed inside in cabins or lounges, to avoid the freezing weather on the boat deck. Those who followed orders and went out to the boats balked at shoving off into the wide ocean on a freezing night in a small lifeboat. They would much rather take their chances on the mighty floating fortress. Even when they began to realize the serious

WOMEN, CHILDREN, AND WEALTHY FIRST

The unwritten code of the sea was that women and children were to go first, along with a few crew members to take charge of each boat. That appeared to be in force on the *Titanic*. When the numbers of dead and surviving passengers were sorted out, however, it appeared that there was a second standard at play. About 75 percent of the passengers riding in third class died. The death rate for first-class passengers was about half that—38 percent. Not even children were able to overcome the class barrier. All but one of the twenty-three children booked in first or second class survived the accident. Yet twenty-six of the seventy-six children in third class died, while a number of first-class men survived. While money might not buy everything, it appeared it could buy a passenger a seat in a lifeboat.

The real story behind the death gap between first and third class, however, proved to be more complicated. True, there were passengers and crew aboard the *Titanic* who believed that upper-class people had priority over those of lower classes. There were reports of crew actually blocking third-class passengers from going up to where the boats were loading.

But the main reason for the difference in survival rates among the classes was location. First-class passengers had access to the more luxurious parts of the ship, which were located higher up in the ship. The only convenient place to store lifeboats was on the top deck. Therefore, first-class passengers had much easier access to them than did third-class passengers whose rooms were far below. In addition, the passages between third class and first class were normally locked to make sure that those who used first-class facilities were those who paid for them. In the confusion after the collision, some of these gates were never unlocked. Even when gates were unlocked, many third-class passengers could not navigate their way through the maze of halls and stairways to find the upper deck. Those passengers caught behind these gates never had a chance. By failing to arrange a plan for evacuation, the crew of the *Titanic* had doomed them to an icy death.

trouble the *Titanic* was in, it took a great deal of courage for them to step out into a small boat swinging from a creaking davit one hundred feet above the water.

As the reality of the situation set in, however, the situation changed from too few people wanting to enter the boats to too many. Chaos and confusion reigned. No one had been assigned to any particular lifeboat. Since there had been no lifeboat drill and, indeed, not even a discussion of lifeboat procedures, no one knew where to go or what to do. Without any rehearsed plan of evacuation, the officers had to make up the rules as they went along while crowded on all sides by frightened passengers.

Not surprisingly, the rules were very different depending on which side of the ship you were on. Officer Charles Lightoller, on the port side, allowed only women and children on board, with no exceptions other than a few crew to row the boats. The most famous victim of this policy was John Jacob Astor, perhaps the wealthiest man aboard the ship. When his young wife stepped into a lifeboat, Astor asked if he could join her. Lightoller informed him that women and children only were to go in the

An artist's rendition attempts to portray the scene onboard the Titanic *as passengers congregated at the lifeboats. While loved ones prepare to part, a young woman refuses to board a lifeboat.*

boats—no exceptions. Had Astor tried to board on the other side of the boat, where Officer Murdoch did not strictly enforce this policy, he might well have gotten off the *Titanic*.

The passengers' responses to the crisis ranged from quiet courage to selfish desperation. On the one hand, many gallantly refused spots aboard the lifeboats so that others could go. On the other hand, a few panicky groups tried to force their way onto boats, particularly when they realized how few lifeboats were aboard the *Titanic*. Officers had to drive them away by firing warning shots from their pistols. A few men had to be dragged out of lifeboats so that women and children could board. Fistfights and wrestling matches were common.

HALF-EMPTY BOATS

The greatest tragedy in the loading of the lifeboats was that many of them went off half empty. Again, the *Titanic* officials' failure to plan for disaster was responsible. Wrongly assuming that the davits could not hold a boat filled to capacity, officers sent boats over the side with as few as twelve people in them. They gave instructions that passengers were to go to a lower deck and board the boats from the cargo ports as they were lowered into the water.

Thanks to poor communication, damage to the ship, and general disorganization, this never happened. Many passengers did as they were told only to find the boats rowing away without picking up anyone else. Others could not find their way through the maze of halls to where they were supposed to go. A crew of six went below with orders to open gates to the cargo ports. They were never seen again—most likely washed away by swirling waters rising through the lower regions of the *Titanic*. Still other passengers tried to get to the cargo ports only to discover that these were already under water.

Then there was the matter of the barriers. Obviously, first-class luxuries such as the pool, lounges, French cafe, and gym were only for those who paid for them. Those who paid third-class fares were not entitled to those facilities. If the passengers were able to freely mingle through the ship, the *Titanic*'s officials would have had a difficult time constantly monitoring who had a right to be in first-class facilities and who did not. Therefore, a system of metal mesh barriers was put in place to keep the classes separate. These barriers greatly restricted movement throughout the ship.

TALES OF COURAGE

The desperate situation of the sinking *Titanic* tested the character of each and every person on board. Many responded with remarkable courage and dignity. Among these were Isidor and Ida Straus, whose story is recounted in many books on the *Titanic*. The Strauses had struggled for years to build Macy's department store into the largest of its kind in the world.

As the call came for women to enter the lifeboats, Ida Straus seemed uncertain what to do. At one point she nearly entered lifeboat 8. Then she changed her mind. The ship's officers tried to persuade her to get into the boat, but she refused. "I've always stayed with my husband," she declared, "so why should I leave him now?"

Some friends urged Isidor Straus to solve the problem by getting into the boat with her. They argued that no one would object to a re-spected old gentleman like him entering the boat. This time it was his turn to refuse. He would not go before any of the other men. The Strauses were last seen sitting on deck chairs, determined to meet their end together.

While a number of surviving passengers were able to relate the Straus story, no one lived to tell of the most courageous men aboard the *Titanic*, the engineers. Far down in the depths of the ship, Chief Engineer Joseph Bell and his crew fought a losing battle against the ocean that was engulfing them. They worked tirelessly to keep steam going to provide power for the pumps and to keep the lights burning. Had they not, the *Titanic* would have sunk sooner and the darkness would have multiplied the chaos that surrounded the lifeboat loading. None of the engineers survived.

Perhaps the most incredible display of courage was the story told by Walter Lord in *A Night to Remember* of an unknown swimmer who approached lifeboat B. At least thirty others had swum to this over-turned raft after the *Titanic* sank. They were crowded onto what amounted to little more than an air mattress that was barely afloat.

When the swimmer approached, some raft occupants shouted frantically that they were already overloaded and had room for no more. Instead of clawing his way onto what was his only chance for survival, endangering those already there, the swimmer kicked away from the raft. Without a trace of bitterness, he called out, "Good luck, God bless you," as he swam into the darkness to meet his fate.

The result of this frantic, uncoordinated effort to fill the lifeboats and rafts was that only about seven hundred people made it into the boats. Two collapsible boats fell into the sea with no one in them. Altogether, the lifeboats floated near the *Titanic* with space for perhaps five hundred people who were now trapped aboard the sinking liner. One of the crew scoffed, "If we are sending boats away, they might just as well put some people in them."[24]

One of *Titanic's* half-empty lifeboats.

THE GREAT SHIP SINKS

All of the people trapped aboard the doomed liner had time to ponder their fate and prepare for the end. At around 2 A.M. Captain Smith began spreading the word that from here on, it was every man for himself. No reliable reports tell how he met his end.

Perhaps the most flamboyant response was that of American multimillionaire Ben Guggenheim. After learning that the *Titanic* had no chance of surviving, Guggenheim retired to his suite. When he came out a few minutes later, he and his servant were wearing their fanciest clothes and looked for all the world as if they were on their way to a formal dinner. If he had to die, Guggenheim planned to go like a gentleman. "I am willing to remain and play the man's game if there are not enough boats for more than women and children," he declared. "No woman shall be left aboard this ship because Ben Guggenheim was a coward."[25]

As ocean water filled the *Titanic's* forward compartments, its weight caused the bow to dip beneath the surface. The lower the bow sank, the higher the stern rose. The three giant screw propellers cleared the water and soared ever higher. Passengers who had been retreating from the sinking bow to the raised stern grabbed whatever solid objects they could find to keep from sliding down to their deaths. Eventually the stern towered above the sea at a forty-five-degree angle from the surface, reaching a height of a twenty-story building. The forward smokestack broke loose and fell, crushing many people, including John Jacob Astor.

Without water beneath it to provide support, the ship's frame could not hold up against the stress estimated to reach fifteen tons per square inch. The bow ripped apart from the stern near the waterline and quickly plunged into the sea. Freed from the

The final moments of the Titanic *are captured in this 1912 painting. Lifeboats and swimmers attempt to flee the sinking ocean liner as its sinking bow causes its stern to lift out of the water.*

weight of the flooded compartments, the stern dropped back down until it was nearly level. But water gushed into the gaping hole left when the bow broke off. Again, the weight of the water coming into one side tipped the remaining piece of the ship until it was almost completely on end, propellers facing the sky. For a few moments it held that position. Then it began its last slide toward its final resting place at the bottom of the ocean, thirteen thousand feet beneath the surface.

At 2:20 A.M., two and a half hours after it had struck the iceberg, the *Titanic* was gone. It had lasted less than five days into its first voyage. In its place was a harrowing nightmare. Those shivering in their lifeboats heard the cries of despair and pleas for help from hundreds of freezing passengers and crew who floated in the darkness. Several dozen swimmers made it to the two empty collapsible lifeboats. One boat returned to rescue a few survivors.

Over the next half hour, the cries gradually died away as the icy Atlantic Ocean claimed one victim after another. By the time the *Carpathia* arrived, shortly after 4:00 A.M., anyone still in the water was long dead from exposure. The *Titanic* was gone and so were the lives of more than fifteen hundred people.

WHAT WENT WRONG

At first, news from the disaster site was sketchy. As the *Carpathia* carried the *Titanic*'s survivors to the North American shore, rumors of all kinds filled the air. The first newspaper reports said that the great ship had sunk but that all passengers had been rescued. When the truth became known, the public was stunned almost beyond comprehension.

The disaster made no sense. Wasn't the *Titanic* the most modern ship ever built? Didn't it dwarf the other vessels in the sea? Hadn't engineering experts pronounced it "virtually unsinkable"? People demanded to know how this disaster could have happened and who was at fault.

Those two questions have been asked repeatedly throughout the past eight decades. Engineering experts and *Titanic* buffs have been engaged in a seemingly endless struggle to nail down all the answers. Some of their proposed answers are commonly accepted, others hotly debated.

SPEED KILLS

The most commonly accepted explanation for the disaster is that the *Titanic* was going too fast. According to the British Board of Trade, which conducted one of the two major investigations that took place after the disaster, the tragedy was "brought about by the excess speed at which the ship was being navigated."[26] Obviously, had the *Titanic* been traveling at a slower speed, it would have had a much better chance of avoiding the iceberg, and the impact would have been far less severe upon striking the iceberg.

The great British explorer Ernest Shackleton, who spent many years sailing the icy seas of Antarctica, was aghast at how fast the *Titanic* was steaming through an ice field. No one disputes that the *Titanic* was traveling at a speed greater than twenty knots. Shackleton's rule of thumb was that any time a ship was traveling in an area where icebergs were reported, it should slow to no more than three or four knots. The *Californian*, sailing in the same ice field as the *Titanic*, had seen fit to stop altogether until daylight.

If reckless speed was the main cause of the disaster, then the blame rests squarely on the shoulders of Captain Smith, although some claimed he was under orders from Bruce Ismay, the president of White Star line.

This explanation, however, is far from the whole story because it leaves some important questions hanging. Smith had a reputation for being one of the outstanding sea captains of his time. He had more experience piloting ocean liners than just about any person alive and could point with pride to his remarkable record for passenger safety. Why would such a man at the very end of his career decide to risk the lives of over twenty-two hundred people by commanding his ship in a reckless fashion?

Famed explorer Ernest Shackleton, an experienced navigator of Antarctica's dangerous seas, blamed the disaster on the Titanic's *reckless speed.*

Most likely, he took no more chances on this trip than he normally had throughout his career. He was probably sailing the way he always had. Furthermore, he was probably doing what the majority of sea captains did when faced with similar circumstances: He maintained a brisk speed while posting lookouts whose job it was to spot icebergs. Once an iceberg was spotted, he likely would have slowed down until the danger was past.

The fate of the *Titanic* may indicate that the standard practice of traveling swiftly until icebergs were spotted was unsafe. But the safety record before that incident gave Smith no cause for concern. He had never had a problem avoiding icebergs. Others in his business had experienced no problem avoiding icebergs. J. H. Biles, a professor at Glasgow University in Scotland, testified shortly after the tragedy that in the entire history of North Atlantic shipping, "We have never heard of a ship being lost by a collision with an iceberg."[27] Why should it have happened to the *Titanic* when countless other ships had been running through ice fields for years without any problem?

WHERE WERE THE BINOCULARS?

Fred Fleet, the lookout who spotted the iceberg, survived the disaster. But he often wished he had not. He was haunted to the end of his days by accusations that, had he been more alert, he would have spotted the iceberg sooner and the tragedy would have been avoided. Fleet maintained that if he had been issued binoculars, which were supposed to be standard equipment on White Star ships, he would have seen the iceberg soon enough to avoid the accident.

White Star officials were certainly at fault in not providing the lookouts with a standard tool of their trade. Still, binoculars of that time were often of poor quality and of limited use, especially at night. Other lookouts admitted that they generally relied on their unaided eyesight to scan the horizon and used binoculars only to get a better view of objects that caught their attention.

INADEQUATE SAFETY FEATURES

Despite the widespread trumpeting of the *Titanic* as one of the safest ships ever built, critics point to a glaring flaw in its design—the shallow bulkheads. These barriers, which were supposed to seal off compartments and so contain leakage to a small section of the ship, did not do the job. What was the point of constructing walls with watertight doors to contain the water if the water

A diagram from the investigation into the Titanic *disaster reveals that the ship's bulkheads were too shallow to act as barriers against incoming water. This obvious engineering flaw allowed the ship to quickly fill with water after the collision.*

could rise over the tops of these walls and spill into the next compartment? Author Anthony Burton states flatly, "If the bulkheads had risen the full height of the vessel, she would have remained afloat a good deal longer—long enough to save hundreds of lives."[28] Some experts believe that, with higher bulkheads, the *Titanic* possibly could even have contained the damage well enough to be towed into port.

To those who argued that building bulkheads that high in a ship was not practical, critics pointed to the *Great Eastern*, a ship built more than fifty years before the *Titanic*, that had such bulkheads.

THE *GREAT EASTERN:* SAFER THAN THE *TITANIC*

Though the *Titanic* was widely viewed as the ultimate in ship strength and safety, passengers would have been safer sailing on a ship built more than half a century earlier. Unlike the *Titanic*, the *Great Eastern was* virtually unsinkable.

Whereas the *Titanic* was divided into sixteen watertight compartments, the *Great Eastern* was a honeycomb of fifty compartments. Not only were its bulkheads built across the width of the ship, but it had two bulkheads that divided the ship along its length. Furthermore, the bulkheads were built up to thirty feet above the waterline, more than four times as high as those of the *Titanic*. These safety features made moving around the ship difficult. The crew had to do a great deal of climbing to get from one part of the ship to the other.

But the emphasis on safety paid off. On August 27, 1862, the *Great Eastern* was passing near the east end of Long Island, New York, when the crew heard a crunching sound. An inspection uncovered no leaks, but Captain Walter Paton hired a diver to see if there was any damage. The diver found that the ship had run into an uncharted ledge of rock. This rock had torn a huge hole—eighty-three feet long and nine feet wide—in the ship's outer iron shell. In terms of the amount of water this let in, the accident was very similar to that of the *Titanic*. Yet its compartments were able to contain the damage well enough for the *Great Eastern* to make it to port, where it was repaired. In his book *The Iron Ship,* Ewan Corlett says, "It is reasonable to surmise that had she been substituted for the *Titanic* in 1912, she would have survived the accident."

The designers of the *Titanic* also had another safety option that they could have used, but did not, to limit the damage from leaks. The *Titanic's* bulkheads all stretched across the width of the ship. When the water poured in, it filled the compartments across that entire width. Some ships contained longitudinal bulkheads, that is, walls that ran down the length of the ship. The *Mauretania* was designed so that the piles of coal used to feed the boilers were stacked lengthwise along the sides of the ships. Both of these designs were useful in confining the damage from a breech in the hull to the edges of the ship. *Scientific American* speculated that the *Mauretania* might have been able to survive the collision that doomed the *Titanic*.

The *Titanic*, however, had no longitudinal bulkheads. Its coal was stacked across the width of the ship. While this was convenient for the stokers, as J. Bernard Walker wrote in *Scientific American*, "From the viewpoint of safety. . . it proved to be fatal."[29]

Once again, however, the *Titanic's* bulkhead design provides only a partial explanation of the ship's fate. While it was certainly possible to design a safer ship, it was not necessarily practical. The *Titanic's* designers could have installed a hundred bulkheads, including longitudinal ones built to the highest deck, to guarantee that any breech in the ship's hull would be contained. But it would have made life impossible for the workers and difficult for the passengers. As the *Great Eastern* proved, there is little point in building a perfectly safe ocean liner if the ship is too expensive to pay for its keep.

Furthermore, the *Titanic's* system of compartments equipped with electromagnetically operated waterproof doors was better than the vast majority of ships on the ocean. It far exceeded government safety standards. Naval architects have argued that modern rules concerning bulkheads do not make present-day liners any safer than the *Titanic*.

FAULTY STEERING

Author George Hilton suggests that the *Titanic* did have a major design flaw but it had nothing to do with the bulkheads. He cites the steering and engine design as the main causes of the disaster. The rudder was of an outdated design that did not work well for a giant ship like the *Titanic*.

More important was the failure to include a reverse gear on the center of the ship's three engines. This caused the ship to

Shipbuilders working on the Titanic *prepare one of its propeller shafts. Some experts contend that flaws in the* Titanic's *steering and engine designs, not its speed, may have been responsible for the liner's disastrous end.*

handle differently from those that the crew had operated before. It is in the steering of the ship, rather than in his ordering of the ship's speed, that Captain Smith may have displayed unforgivable negligence. He apparently took little time to test the ship's handling so that he and his crew could become familiar with the quirks caused by its unusual design. In the ship's brief trials, the crew did not run through the various emergency situations that they might encounter.

When the alarm came from the lookouts that an iceberg was dead ahead, Officer Murdoch had no time to ponder the situation or consult with others. He had to act on instinct. Instinct told him that he needed to do two things: turn as sharply as he could one way or the other to avoid the iceberg and slow the ship's speed to lessen the impact if he could not avoid it.

Therefore, he ordered the crew to turn sharply to the left and throw the engines into reverse. The first part of his order was correct, Hilton points out. But as for the second part, "the consequences of the command could not have been worse."[30] Only the outside engines could be reversed; the center engine simply stopped. Since the rudder was directly behind the center engine, this meant that the stream of water it churned toward the rudder also stopped. The effectiveness of the rudder in causing a change of direction depended on the speed of the water flowing against it. Therefore, by ordering the engines reversed, Murdoch cut back on the *Titanic*'s ability to respond.

During the thirty-eight seconds before collision, the *Titanic* turned only twenty-two degrees to port. Had it been able to turn a full forty degrees, as should have been possible, it would have avoided the collision altogether. According to Hilton, Murdoch should have ordered full reverse on the port (left) screw propeller only. He should have continued full speed ahead on the center and starboard engines. This would have had the same effect as jamming a canoe paddle into the water on one side—the faster the canoe is going, the sharper the turn.

Murdoch had another, less complicated alternative open to him: He could simply have reversed the engines and hit the iceberg head-on. Ironically, even if he had panicked and done

BIZARRE TALE OF THE *TITAN*

Those who believe strongly in psychic powers often cite an almost forgotten book that appeared to describe in detail the tragedy of the *Titanic*. The story, called "Futility," was written by a struggling writer named Morgan Robertson and was first published in a New York magazine.

The plot concerned a luxury ocean liner named the *Titan*. This ship was the largest ever built. It was about eight hundred feet long and was divided into numerous watertight compartments, which led the experts to consider it unsinkable. Like the real *Titanic*, the *Titan* could sail at a top speed of twenty-five knots. In Robertson's story, the *Titan* carried about two thousand people, including many of the fabulously wealthy. Sailing in the Atlantic Ocean in April, it struck an iceberg and sank, and had far too few lifeboats to accommodate everyone on board.

In short, Robertson could be accused of borrowing the entire incident of the *Titanic*'s sinking for his book—except for one fact: "Futility" was published in 1898, long before William Pirrie even dreamed of building the great ship.

nothing, the *Titanic* would have come out much better than it did. A head-on collision, at the speed the *Titanic* was moving, probably would have caused some deaths, especially among those in the front of the boat. However, it would have flooded only two or possibly three of the least vulnerable compartments, and the ship would have stayed afloat.

Of course, Murdoch can hardly be blamed for trying to avoid the collision. Anyone in his place would have done the same. Had he made no effort to turn away from the iceberg, no one would have been congratulating him for having saved the ship and thousands of passengers. Instead, he would have taken the full brunt of the blame for the accident and loss of life and undoubtedly would have lost his job.

SO FEW LIFEBOATS

The one decision that virtually everyone condemned in the most outraged tones was the decision to carry so few lifeboats. Many people, especially the friends and relatives of those who died because they were stranded on the *Titanic*, believed that nearly everyone on board would have been saved had there been lifeboats available to take them.

As with many other criticisms of the *Titanic*'s voyage, however, the matter is not as clear-cut as it at first seemed. White Star officials had provided for more lifeboat capacity than government safety regulations required. A comparison with the fate of a rival luxury ocean liner, the *Lusitania*, demonstrates why the number of lifeboats on board did not necessarily provide any more safety.

The *Lusitania* had carried twenty-two lifeboats and twenty-six collapsible rafts for a total capacity of 2,605 persons. This provided plenty of space for every one of the 1,257 passengers and 712 crew, with room to spare. Yet when a German submarine fired a torpedo into it three years after the *Titanic* disaster, the loss of life was roughly the same proportion as on the *Titanic*. This was because within eighteen minutes of the torpedo striking it, the *Lusitania* was gone. In that time, the crew was able to load and shove off only six lifeboats. Despite ample lifeboat capacity, 1,198 persons died in the tragedy. Many of those who survived were picked out of the water by rescue vessels.

The fast-sinking *Lusitania* scene was far more typical than the fate of the *Titanic*. The passengers and crew of the *Titanic* experienced extraordinarily good luck in boarding the boats the night of the disaster, perhaps the only good bit of luck that befell them during that entire evening. The fact that the *Titanic* lasted so long, longer even than its designer, Thomas Andrews,

expected, was a credit to the engineers and workers of Harland and Wolff. For despite the damage it sustained and the force of the water pouring into it, the *Titanic* remained relatively stable from side to side. Had the ship tilted severely to one side or the other, boarding the lifeboats would have been extremely difficult. Had it capsized altogether, there would have been only a handful of survivors.

In the vast majority of shipwrecks, the *Titanic*'s crew would not have been able to load any more people into lifeboats than they did. Yet even with the unexpected luxury of all that time, they were not able to get nearly as many people aboard lifeboats as they should.

Certainly, if the *Titanic* had carried more lifeboats, lives would have been saved. But not as many as critics claimed. Even if the *Titanic* had pro-

Titanic stayed relatively upright while sinking. Had it not, loading and lowering the lifeboats would have been more difficult, if not impossible.

vided lifeboat or life raft room for everyone on board, at the rate these were filled, nearly one thousand people would have been left to die on the *Titanic* anyway. And this was under exceptionally favorable lifeboat-loading circumstances.

Furthermore, Hilton argues that adding lifeboats could be more of a danger than a blessing to passengers. He cites the case of the *Eastland,* a large passenger steamer. In the aftermath of the *Titanic* disaster, the *Eastland* was forced to abide by new government regulations requiring all ships to carry enough lifeboats to provide space for every person on board. On July 24, 1915, the *Eastland* was ferrying employees of the Western Electric Company in Chicago to a picnic. Suddenly the ship rolled over on its side into the Chicago River. Eight hundred forty-four people died.

Crowds stand atop the Eastland, *which capsized shortly after it was required to carry additional lifeboats. Investigators maintain that the extra weight from the lifeboats made the ship top-heavy.*

According to Hilton's investigation, the *Eastland* was stable when it was built. But the requirement to add more lifeboats on the top deck made it top-heavy. Far from preventing deaths, the extra lifeboats actually caused them.

THE SHIP THAT STOOD IDLY BY

The *Californian* was close enough to the *Titanic* that it should have been able to rescue many of the passengers aboard. The *Californian's* officers clearly saw the flares sent up by the *Titanic* crew to summon help. Some of them suspected that the *Titanic* was in trouble and brought their concerns to the ship's captain, Stanley Lord.

Captain Lord responded by doing as little as possible, short of ignoring the entire thing. He chose to signal the *Titanic* with lamps, which the crew of the *Titanic* was in a poor position to see. When this produced no response, he let the matter drop.

Lord claimed his ship was too far away for it to have been the one seen by the *Titanic's* officers. His defenders have argued that the flares were not a recognized distress signal. Given the *Titanic's* reputation as invincible, a captain could easily have mistaken them for fireworks and assumed the *Titanic* was throwing some kind of lavish party for its high-priced guests.

However, Lord's employer, the Leyland line, immediately fired him for his indifferent response to the *Titanic's* plight. Inquiries into the disaster blamed him for laziness bordering on criminal negligence. Although Lord spent the rest of his life trying to justify his actions and clear his name, he remains one of the most widely criticized culprits in the *Titanic* disaster.

A Dream Too Big?

Many people wondered if the *Titanic* disaster was the result of humans getting too proud for their own good. Several experts have observed that the *Titanic's* accident highlighted a major flaw in Pirrie's dream of the fleet of giant liners: He had built ships that were too big for the existing facilities. While this flaw did not directly affect the events that took place, it certainly would have had the *Titanic* managed to limp into port. According to one expert, "Even if the *Titanic* had stayed afloat and been towed to Halifax, she would have been a total loss."[31]

This was because there were no facilities in North America large enough to take on and repair such a monster ship. In fact, even if the wounded *Titanic* made it back to the Harland and Wolff yard in Belfast, the chances of repair were poor. Riding low in the water, the ship would have been too heavy to pull up onto the dry dock.

When designing the Titanic *(right) and the* Olympic *(left), Harland and Wolff failed to realize that these ships would be too large to dock at existing repair facilities.*

But more important, by building such a huge ship, William Pirrie entrusted thousands of lives to a single, untested floating fortress. This was practically an invitation to a major disaster. A smaller ship striking an iceberg might go down with several dozen or even a couple hundred casualties. While this would have been tragic, it would not have had the horrific impact of the more than fifteen hundred deaths aboard the *Titanic.*

BAD LUCK

While the owners, designers, and operators of the *Titanic* made many mistakes that contributed to the disaster, the catastrophe would not have happened without an incredible string of bad luck.

The weather conditions could not have been worse. Had the ocean been foggy, the crew would have had to slow down, knowing they could not spot icebergs at any great distance. Had they been sailing in stormy weather, they also would have slowed down. But since the weather was clear, they sped on, assuming they could spot icebergs without difficulty. Unfortunately, with no moon in the sky, visibility was reduced. Because there was not a breath of a breeze, the ocean was perfectly still. This deprived lookouts of one of the tell-tale clues as to the existence of ice—the waves breaking against it.

Harland and Wolff designers pore over plans for the Titanic. *They could not foresee a situation in which six of the ship's compartments would flood simultaneously.*

The timing of the accident proved disastrous. Had the wireless operator aboard the *Californian* stayed at his key another fifteen minutes, or had the *Titanic* accident occurred that much earlier, he would have heard the distress call. In that case, nearly everyone could have been saved. The *Titanic* also had the misfortune of colliding when it happened to be too far away from another ship (other than the *Californian*) for help to arrive on time.

The evasive action the *Titanic* had to take to avoid the iceberg happened to be a maneuver that the ship was not designed to perform. The ship then collided with an iceberg, an event that insurance experts figured was a million to one shot. Not only did it strike the iceberg, but the *Titanic* struck it at exactly the worst possible angle. The designers of the *Titanic* had never planned for a situation in which six compartments took on water at the same time, for a very good reason. In the entire history of ocean navigation, there is no record of any other ship suffering a side-swipe blow that damaged nearly three hundred feet of its length, as did the *Titanic*.

In the words of *Scientific American,* "We very much doubt if any other possible accident of wind, weather, or collision with another ship could have sunk the *Titanic.*"[32]

Finally, the ship happened to be sailing at a time and place where the water was extremely cold. Had the accident occurred in warmer waters, the hundreds of *Titanic* passengers and crew who were floating in life belts could well have survived the couple of hours it took for the *Carpathia* to arrive.

THE MYSTERY FACTOR

One thing that investigators puzzled over for years was exactly what damage the *Titanic* sustained. Engineer Edward Wilding of Harland and Wolff collected eyewitness evidence about how long it took water to reach various decks on the ship. From that information, he calculated the rate at which water entered the ship. The fact that six compartments were breached indicated that the *Titanic* suffered damage along nearly three hundred feet of its length. Using this estimate, Wilding then calculated the size of the gash that would have allowed water to enter the *Titanic* at the rate estimated. According to his figures, the hole could not have been larger than three-quarters of an inch. Wilding testified that it was unlikely that an iceberg could have opened such a long, razor-thin slit in a one-inch-thick steel hull. Something other than a simple gash, he concluded, had damaged the *Titanic*.

Over the years, many people speculated about what this damage must have been. Some suggested that the collision could have burst open a long seam of rivets. This led to suspicions that the *Titanic* was done in by sabotage. Could Irish workers at Harland and Wolff have been so embittered by disputes between the Irish and Great Britain that they purposely slacked off on the quality of their work for the British ship?

There has never been any evidence, however, to support such a suggestion. The *Olympic* was built by the same workers

SAFETY RULES PROMPTED BY THE *TITANIC'S* SINKING

The greatest public outcry over the sinking was the shortage of life-boats. The U.S. and British governments immediately set up requirements that ships be equipped with lifeboat space for every person aboard. New regulations requiring lifeboat instructions and drills were also introduced. The *Titanic's* sinking also led to alterations in the height of bulkheads on many ships, including the *Olympic.*

As a result of the agonizing inability to contact the *Californian,* new regulations were set up requiring all sailing ships to have someone monitoring the wireless twenty-four hours a day. When the *Carpathia* sailed into New York with the *Titanic's* survivors, amateur radio operators clogged the airwaves, asking for news and reporting rumors. This made vital communications difficult. As a result, the U.S. government set up the Federal Communications Commission to regulate the use of the airwaves.

The most effective change inspired by the *Titanic* disaster was the attitude toward icebergs. From that time on, all ships took seriously reports of icebergs in their area and slowed down even before they spotted them. The United States and Great Britain, supported by fourteen other nations, also set up the International Ice Patrol. This organization uses ships and airplanes to scout and report on the number and size of icebergs in the shipping lanes. In some cases, the U.S. Coast Guard sends ships to tow some of the more dangerous bergs to a safe place.

Since the sinking of the *Titanic,* only two ships are known to have struck ice and sunk. One occurred during World War II, when the Ice Patrol was temporarily disbanded. The other involved a Danish passenger ship that was designed especially to sail in icy North Atlantic waters in the winter. Since other ships avoided sailing the route taken by this ship in January 1959, the Ice Patrol was not yet on duty for that year. On January 30, one day before the Ice Patrol resumed its work, the ship collided with an iceberg and sank. All passengers were lost.

Both of these tragedies highlight the effectiveness of the Ice Patrol. When it has been in operation, not a single life has been lost to ice collisions.

and held up admirably. Furthermore, many of the workers' friends in Belfast sailed as crew members aboard the *Titanic.*

For more than half a century, it seemed unlikely anyone would ever know exactly what damage the iceberg caused. After all, the *Titanic* was buried out of reach beneath two and a half miles of ocean.

Epilogue: *Titanic* Found

Seventy years after the sinking of the *Titanic,* underwater technology had advanced to the point where researchers could probe the deepest trenches of the ocean. In the summer of 1985, a joint U.S.–French expedition set out to find the wreckage of the *Titanic.* Beginning at roughly the spot from which the last distress messages from the *Titanic* were sent, the team sent an unmanned search vessel called the *Argo* to the ocean bottom. For a month and a half, this deep-sea submarine combed the ocean bottom with its cameras. Finally, on September 1, researchers monitoring the screen in the control room on a surface ship saw the ghostly shape of an abandoned wreck appear. The *Argo* had found the *Titanic.*

For days, the *Argo* took thousands of photographs of the *Titanic,* from a wide variety of angles. Unfortunately, much of the starboard hull of the *Titanic* had been buried on impact in sixty feet of ocean sediment. It was impossible to get a good look at the section that struck the iceberg. In the section of hull that was visible, researcher Robert Ballard noted some buckled metal plates and strong evidence that rivets had popped. Otherwise, there was a curious lack of obvious damage. This rekindled talk of sloppy construction and perhaps sabotage.

Robert Ballard, the oceanographer who discovered the sunken Titanic.

But the undersea photographs of the *Titanic* revealed another bizarre twist to the mystery. Metal is a somewhat flexible material compared with such things as rock and ice. It tends to bend and stretch on severe impact. An iceberg could not slit open an inch-thick steel plate like a razor slicing through plastic. Instead, one would expect it to crush the hull inward until it opened up a hole. Yet as far as could be seen from the photographs, the metal plates did not bend inward.

Then in 1991, a team of scientists and engineers led by Canadian Steve Blasco discovered a ten-inch chunk of metal lying near the *Titanic.* It was obvious from the thickness of the piece that it had broken off from the hull. The edges appeared jagged, like what you would expect on a piece of broken china.

Again, given the nature of metal, this discovery seemed strange. One would expect to find holes in the hull where it ripped apart under pressure of the collision. Why would a piece of metal break completely away from the rest of the hull? And why would its edges look like those of a piece of some shattered inflexible material?

Experts familiar with the properties of steel thought they knew the answer to this riddle. One of them, Ken KarisAllen, had a chance to test his theory on this piece of hull in 1994. KarisAllen conducted an experiment in which he subjected a piece of modern, high-quality steel to a violent impact. As expected, the steel bent and stretched at the impact point, but did not break. He then performed the same test on the piece of *Titanic* hull. This steel shattered like glass.

The test confirmed that the *Titanic* was likely a victim of brittle fracture. This is a property of metal that causes it, on rare occasions, to break apart rather than bend under stress. There have even been cases in which steel has been known to suddenly shatter without any apparent reason.

Brittle fracture was not unknown at the time of the *Titanic* disaster (there is a recorded case of it occurring as early as 1879). But it was poorly understood. Engineers did not know, for example, that a high sulfur content makes steel brittle. The amount of sulfur in the *Titanic*'s steel plate was high even compared with

In August 1998, researchers recovered this hull section from the Titanic. *This recovery, like previous ones, shows signs of brittle fractures in the steel.*

other steel made in its time. Engineers merely tested the steel to find the maximum stress it could withstand before it broke, and if it passed that test, it was considered fit for construction.

The steel used in the *Titanic*, apparently, was unsafe. As KarisAllen noted, "To make present-day high quality steel that brittle, I'd have to lower its temperature to minus 60 or 70 degrees Celsius." The people traveling in luxury aboard the *Titanic* thought they were sailing on a practically indestructible steel giant. In fact, they were sailing on a very fragile craft. The cold waters of the North Atlantic further weakened *Titanic's* steel plate. Steve Blasco summed up the fate of the *Titanic* by saying, "Shipbuilding technology had outstripped metallurgy technology."[33]

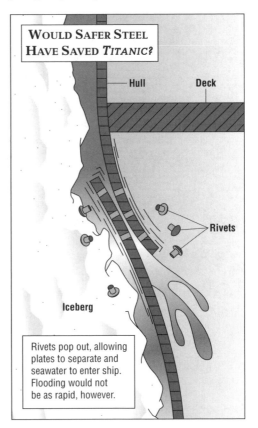

WOULD SAFER STEEL HAVE SAVED *TITANIC?*

Hull

Deck

Rivets

Iceberg

Rivets pop out, allowing plates to separate and seawater to enter ship. Flooding would not be as rapid, however.

Had the steel plate been up to the standards of modern construction, it might have absorbed most of the energy of the collision with the iceberg. It would have bent and stretched; perhaps a hole or two would have been punched through. Very likely some rivets would have popped out, causing the seams between plates to pull apart and let water in. Perhaps the leak would have been bad enough that the *Titanic* would not have been able to reach port. But there seems a good chance that the ship would have been able to stay afloat long enough for the *Carpathia* and other rescue ships to arrive.

In 1995, researchers were able to probe into the mud covering the *Titanic's* starboard side. They confirmed that there was no long, deep gash. Incredibly, the great ship was done in by a series of six holes with a total area of only twelve square feet.

While information is still being collected on the *Titanic*, we now have a good idea why the *Titanic* sank. The human mistakes were many. Harland and Wolff and White Star tried to build a ship that was beyond the technology of the times. In

Despite the decades since its occurrence, the Titanic *disaster continues to be a story that both fascinates and horrifies. Here, an image of the* Titanic's *rust-covered bow dominates the screen at a 1991 IMAX film presentation about the ill-fated ship.*

order to make the ship attractive and economical, they compromised on some safety features such as lifeboats and high bulkheads. Captain Smith ran the ship too fast, considering the iceberg danger and the weather conditions. The crew was not prepared for an emergency. Smith and the crew did not take the necessary time to learn how the *Titanic* handled in all situations. Therefore, the wrong orders were given when the ship tried to avoid the iceberg. Once the accident took place, there was no well-rehearsed system for evacuating the ship.

None of these errors was totally responsible for the disaster. But when an extraordinary streak of bad luck struck the *Titanic*, each contributed to the horrifying spectacle that continues to fascinate people today.

NOTES

Introduction

1. Quoted in Susan Wels, Titanic: *Legacy of the World's Greatest Ocean Liner.* New York: Time-Life, 1997, p. 86.

2. Quoted in Walter Lord, *A Night to Remember.* New York: Holt, Rinehart, and Winston, 1955, p. 32.

Chapter 1: Birth of the Monster Ships

3. Robert Albion, *Five Centuries of Famous Ships.* New York: McGraw-Hill, 1978, p. 170.

4. Albion, *Five Centuries of Famous Ships,* p. 217.

5. Michael Davie, Titanic: *The Death and Life of a Legend.* New York: Knopf, 1987, p. 9.

Chapter 2: Building the *Titanic*

6. Quoted in Wels, Titanic, p. 12.

7. Quoted in Terry Coleman, *The Liners: A History of the North Atlantic Crossing.* London: Penguin, 1976, p. 39.

8. Quoted in Lord, *A Night to Remember,* p. 36.

9. Davie, Titanic, p. 67.

10. Quoted in Anthony Burton, *The Rise and Fall of British Shipbuilding.* London: Constable, 1994, p. 131.

11. Burton, *The Rise and Fall of British Shipbuilding,* p. 119.

12. Quoted in Lord, *A Night to Remember,* p. 173.

13. Quoted in Davie, Titanic, p. 14.

Chapter 3: Seeds of Disaster

14. Quoted in Charles Hirschberg, "The Tragedy of the *Titanic*," *Life,* June 1997, p. 68.

15. Quoted in Lord, *A Night to Remember,* p. 50.

16. Quoted in Wels, Titanic, p. 44.

17. George W. Hilton, Eastland: *Legacy of the Titanic.* Stanford, CA: Stanford University Press, 1995, p. 1.

18. Hilton, Eastland, p. 3.

19. Quoted in Davie, Titanic, p. 9.

Chapter 4: The Fateful Night

20. Quoted in Hirschberg, "The Tragedy of the *Titanic*," p. 67.

21. Quoted in Hirschberg, "The Tragedy of the *Titanic*," p. 67.

22. Quoted in Paul J. Quinn, Titanic *at Two.* Saco, ME: Fantail, 1997, p. 67.

23. Quoted in Quinn, Titanic *at Two*, p. 67.

24. Quoted in Lord, *A Night to Remember*, p. 64.

25. Quoted in Wyn Craig Wade, Titanic: *End of a Dream*. New York: Penguin, 1986, p. 57.

Chapter 5: What Went Wrong

26. Quoted in Coleman, *The Liners*, p. 54.

27. Quoted in Davie, Titanic, p. 191.

28. Burton, *The Rise and Fall of British Shipbuilding*, p. 163.

29. J. Bernard Walker, "The 'Unsinkable Ship,'" *Scientific American*, May 11, 1912, p. 418.

30. Hilton, Eastland, p. 2.

31. "The Monster Ship," *Nation*, May 9, 1912, p. 454.

32. "Light Out of a Dark Tragedy," *Scientific American*, April 27, 1912, p. 381.

Epilogue: *Titanic* Found

33. Quoted in Robert Gannon, "The *Titanic*'s Final Secret," *Reader's Digest*, August 1995, pp. 158, 160.

GLOSSARY

bow: The front part of the ship.

bulkhead: A wall or partition that divides a ship into compartments, used for support and for confining leaks to a small portion of the ship.

davit: A crane from which a lifeboat hangs suspended by ropes over the side of the ship.

deck: A floor on the ship.

gross tonnage: A measurement of a ship's weight.

knot: A shortened form of the term *nautical mile*, it is a unit of measure equal to 1.15 miles. When the *Titanic* was traveling at a top speed of twenty-two knots, this was equal to roughly twenty-five miles per hour.

port: The left side of the ship.

starboard: The right side of the ship.

stern: The rear part of the ship.

For Further Reading

Michael Davie, Titanic: *The Death and Life of a Legend.* New York: Knopf, 1987. Davie provides background into some of the main characters behind the building of the *Titanic* as well as a clear account of the ship's disastrous voyage.

Walter Lord, *A Night to Remember.* New York: Holt, Rinehart, and Winston, 1955. This is probably the best known book on the *Titanic* disaster, told through the words of eyewitnesses.

Paul J. Quinn, Titanic *at Two.* Saco, ME: Fantail, 1997. This book provides more minute-by-minute detail of the final moments of the *Titanic.*

Neil Schlager, ed., *When Technology Fails.* Detroit: Gale Research, 1994. A collection of reports about great disasters, including the sinking of the *Titanic,* from the angle of miscalculations and mistakes in technology.

Susan Wels, Titanic: *Legacy of the World's Greatest Ocean Liner.* New York: Time-Life, 1997. A lavishly illustrated, detailed history of the *Titanic.*

ADDITIONAL WORKS CONSULTED

Robert Albion, *Five Centuries of Famous Ships.* New York: McGraw-Hill, 1978. The dean of American maritime historians examines the history of the rise of steam over sails.

Anthony Burton, *The Rise and Fall of British Shipbuilding.* London: Constable, 1994. Looks at the British shipyard workers and industry leaders who were at the peak of their power and influence during the time when the *Titanic* was built.

Terry Coleman, *The Liners: A History of the North Atlantic Crossing.* London: Penguin, 1976. Coleman includes a great deal of illustration in his description of the Atlantic liners that vied for prominence beginning in the later nineteenth century.

Ewan Corlett, *The Iron Ship.* New York: Arco, 1975. This book tells the story of how iron supplanted wood in the building of ocean liners, focusing heavily on Brunel's innovative *Great Britain*.

Paul Heyde, *Titanic Legacy: Disaster as Media Event and Myth.* Westport, CT: Praeger, 1995. A media historian looks at the publicity surrounding the sinking of the *Titanic* and probes how the reaction to the disaster influenced our culture.

George W. Hilton, Eastland: *Legacy of the* Titanic. Stanford, CA: Stanford University Press, 1995. Although this book is primarily concerned with a different maritime catastrophe, it probes behind popular criticism to the real causes of the *Titanic* disaster.

A. A. Hoehling, *Ships That Changed History.* Lanham, MD: Madison Books, 1992. This historian focuses on a few influential ships, with detailed analyses of the *Great Eastern* and the *Lusitania*.

Walter Lord, *The Night Lives On.* New York: William Morrow, 1986. Lord wrote this as a sequel to his acclaimed first book to reexamine unanswered questions surrounding the *Titanic* disaster.

John Maxtone-Graham, *Liners to the Sun.* New York: Macmillan, 1985. An affectionate look at the bygone days of ocean liners by a man who traveled on many of them.

Wyn Craig Wade, Titanic: *End of a Dream*. New York: Penguin, 1986. Another detailed account of the circumstances surrounding the building, launching, and sinking of the *Titanic*.

Periodicals Consulted

Robert Ballard, "How the 'Unsinkable' Ship Sank," *National Geographic*, October 1987.

Robert Gannon, "The *Titanic*'s Final Secret," *Reader's Digest*, August 1995.

Robert Gannon, "What Really Sank the *Titanic*," *Popular Science*, February 1995.

Charles Hirschberg, "The Tragedy of the *Titanic*," *Life*, June 1997.

"Light Out of a Dark Tragedy," *Scientific American*, April 27, 1912.

"The Monster Ship," *Nation*, May 9, 1912.

J. Bernard Walker, "The 'Unsinkable Ship,'" *Scientific American*, May 11, 1912.

INDEX

PICTURE CREDITS

ABOUT THE AUTHOR

Nathan Aaseng is the author of more than 140 books for young readers on a wide variety of subjects. More than three dozen of his works have won awards. A former microbiologist with a degree in biology and English from Luther College (Iowa), he currently lives in Eau Claire, Wisconsin, with his wife and four children.